KING TRUTHS

ALVEDA KING

CHARISMA
HOUSE

Most CHARISMA HOUSE BOOK GROUP products are available at special quantity discounts for bulk purchase for sales promotions, premiums, fund-raising, and educational needs. For details, write Charisma House Book Group, 600 Rinehart Road, Lake Mary, Florida 32746, or telephone (407) 333-0600.

KING TRUTHS by Alveda C. King
Published by Charisma House
Charisma Media/Charisma House Book Group
600 Rinehart Road
Lake Mary, Florida 32746
www.charismahouse.com

Cover design by Justin Evans

Visit the author's website at www.alvedaking.com.

Library of Congress Cataloging-in-Publication Data:
An application to register this book for cataloging has been submitted to the Library of Congress.
International Standard Book Number: 978-1-62999-454-3
E-book ISBN: 978-1-62999-455-0

First edition

18 19 20 21 22 — 987654321
Printed in the United States of America

*This book is dedicated to my Creator, my Abba,
the Father of my Lord Jesus Christ, and to the
Holy Spirit.*

*I acknowledge God's grace for the inspiration
and creation of this book, and I thank Him
for blessing me with my biological family, my
church family, and the many friends and sup-
porters who have been part of this journey. May
God forever bless each and every one of you.*

*Finally, to Charisma House—from the founder
to each and every member of the team who has
shared in this labor of love—I say God bless each
and every one of you in every way, forever.*

"I thank my God upon every remembrance of you."
—Philippians 1:3, NKJV

CONTENTS

FOREWORD

S OME YEARS AGO I sat at a roundtable with several African Americans to discuss the issue of civil rights, both past and present. Around the table we had ministry leaders of some stature, such as Bishop Harry Jackson, apostle Willie F. Wooten, revivalist Sean Smith, prayer leaders Will and Dehavilland Ford, and the author of this book, Alveda King. I have the honor and privilege of calling each of them dear friends.

I thought I knew each one well, but as I listened to the stories of pain they had endured, my eyes were opened. Their lives and families had been profoundly affected by the things they had suffered. Sometimes it seems that you don't really know a person until you know not only who the person is today but also what formed the person into that individual.

That roundtable marked me on a level that is hard to describe. Bishop Jackson told why his family moved north during his grandfather's era. "Times were horrific in the South," he explained. "My father tells of when his father saw bodies swinging from trees—people with his skin color." The family members fled for their very lives to what they hoped would be a somewhat safe haven.

Smith's dad, a highly educated man, was stopped and killed by men that Sean has since found out had connections to the KKK. Ford has shared publicly how she inadvertently threw a snowball at a police car when she was a young girl. The policemen got out of the car, were absolutely irate, and were going to rape her until a passing vehicle made them think better of it.[1]

Alveda opened her heart about how she was part of the 1963 Children's Crusade, when children marched in Birmingham, Alabama, to protest segregation. She recounted that her uncle Martin Luther King Jr. (or Uncle ML, as she affectionately calls him in this book) had not thought the police would turn the dogs on and use water cannons against such young ones. History sadly leaves us with a different scenario. Many of the children were arrested for parading without a permit. They returned to march the next day, and police sprayed them with fire hoses, hit them with batons, and even turned the police dogs upon them.[2]

This is a book filled with truths Alveda King learned from her family during tough times—love instead of hate, forgiveness rather than bitterness. She comes from a legacy of tenacious reformers who would go to any length to follow God's precepts. She doesn't pretend her family is perfect, but they have known and do know they can go to the One who is and was perfect to receive restoration, forgiveness, and healing.

I believe there are blessings that come from a family line. The hunger to see our society follow God's precepts began even before her uncle ML wrote his letter from a Birmingham jail cell. In fact, upon his birth Martin Luther King Jr. was named Michael King Jr. But in 1934 his father made a historic trip to Germany, where he attended an international conference of Baptist pastors. Michael King became so impressed with what he had learned about the Reformer Martin Luther that he decided to do something dramatic. He changed his name from Michael King to Martin Luther King. Therefore, upon returning home, he also changed his son's name to Martin Luther King Jr., and the rest is history.[3]

Today Alveda King stands upon the shoulders of Martin Luther King, her grandfather. The words she writes in this book are written from the wells dug by her granddaddy; her daddy, who was assassinated one year after her uncle ML; her mother; and other family members. Read every page. You will walk away feeling imbued with a depth of knowledge from her generational heritage. My friend Alveda has earned the right to speak these truths, and I personally know that she lives every word that she writes.

—Cindy Jacobs
Cofounder, Generals International
Dallas, Texas

PREFACE

He [Jesus] said, "To you it has been given to know the secrets of the kingdom of God, but for others they are in parables, so that 'seeing they may not see, and hearing they may not understand.'"

—Luke 8:10, ESV

IN THE MID-1990S I was participating in a prayer meeting at my home church, Believers' Bible Christian Church in Atlanta, Georgia, when I suddenly began to sing aloud, "It pleases the Father to give you the keys; the keys to His kingdom, reach out and receive." The lyrics seemed to bubble up in my spirit, and while there were no visible instruments, it seemed as though heavenly music were playing in the atmosphere. "The Keys Song," born that day, marked the beginning of my awareness of spiritual keys to the kingdom of God.

Nearly two decades later a prophetic artist named Adam Kurrey came to me during a conference and presented to me a painting he had created. He'd named it *Dream of Justice*, and the painting has keys all over it. When he first gave it to me, I didn't connect the dots back to "The Keys Song," but when I began writing this book, I looked back at a note Adam had given me along with the painting. The message was a prophetic word that I had read previously, but this time one sentence seemed to jump off the page at me: "You have accessed by your faith keys to the kingdom that have unlocked doors and places that have been kept blocked for generations."

I finally began to see what God was doing. There truly are keys to the kingdom that will unlock doors and places that have been kept blocked for generations—and that is why God led me to write this book. Now is the time for us to use those divine keys to open the doors.

Within these pages is the revelation of the spiritual keys that God has been birthing into my spirit. These are truths that I have come to live by and that I have seen at work in my family for generations. It is my joy to share these keys with you, and I pray they bless your life as much as they have blessed my and my family's lives.

Artist Adam Kurrey and I pose next to his prophetic painting *Dream of Justice*.

To hear Alveda King's
"The Keys Song,"
scan the QR code
or visit
https://tinyurl.com/TheKeysSong.

INTRODUCTION

And I will give you the keys of the Kingdom of Heaven.
Whatever you forbid [bind or lock] on earth will be
forbidden in heaven, and whatever you permit [loose
or open] on earth will be permitted in heaven.

—MATTHEW 16:19

D O YOU REMEMBER when your parents first gave you a key to your childhood home? How about when you received the key to your first car? Your first office or your first home? Do you remember how you felt? Maybe you felt an awesome sense of responsibility. Maybe for the first time you felt as if you were in charge. Getting the keys to a place or a thing means you have the power and authority to enter and depart at any time. Keys also indicate a certain level of responsibility over the security of a place and its contents. You have keys so you can unlock doors to access what you need.

You probably haven't thought that deeply about your keys in a long time. As time has gone by, maybe you've become used to your keys and even the doors they open. Maybe they've become old hat in your life, and you kind of take them for granted, as some of the excitement of having the keys has worn off.

Just as we have keys in the natural, we have been given a set of spiritual keys that help us unlock the things in the supernatural world that we need to access in our natural world—favor, faith, opportunity, provision, healing, and deliverance from spiritual enemies. Spiritual keys have a level of spiritual authority and power attached to them. I also call these divine keys because they have been given to us by God.

These spiritual keys are not quite like the keys we handle in our natural, everyday lives. The more we submit ourselves to God's design for our lives, the more power we will receive from these divine spiritual keys. And because these keys are multidimensional, they have the propensity to adapt as we gain insight and grow in our spiritual gifts and abilities. Let's break this down some.

The words *key*, *keys*, and *divine keys* are code words in this book. They symbolize ways we access authority and power.

According to an Oxford dictionary, *authority* can take on the following meanings:[1]

- "The power or right to give orders, make decisions, and enforce obedience." (e.g.: "He had absolute authority over his subordinates.") Synonyms: "power, jurisdiction, command, control, charge"

- "The right to act in a specified way, delegated from one person or organization to another." (e.g.: "Military forces have the legal authority to arrest drug traffickers.") Synonyms: "authorization, right, power, mandate, prerogative, license"

- "Official permission; sanction." (e.g.: "The money was spent without [congressional] authority.") Synonyms: "consent, leave, assent"

- "The power to influence others, especially because of one's commanding manner or one's recognized knowledge about something." (e.g.: "He has the natural authority of one who is used to being obeyed.") Synonyms: "power, jurisdiction, command, control, mastery, charge, dominance, dominion, rule, sovereignty, ascendancy, supremacy, domination, influence, sway, control, leverage, power, command, weight"

The word *power* makes an appearance in each of the previous definitions of *authority*. *Power* is a word with broad meaning. As you will see, each of the following definitions of *power* relates to a capacity within which we can express our authority.[2]

- "The ability to do something or act in a particular way" (e.g.: "the power of speech," "his powers of concentration.") Synonyms: "ability, capacity, capability, potential, faculty, competence"

- "The capacity or ability to direct or influence the behaviour of others or the course of events." (e.g.: "She had me in her power.")

- "Physical strength and force exerted by something or someone." (e.g.: "the power of the storm.") Synonyms: "strength, powerfulness, might, force, forcefulness, vigour, energy, powerfulness, potency, strength, force, cogency, persuasiveness"

- "Energy that is produced by mechanical, electrical, or other means [such as spiritual power, in the case of the life of a believer] and used to operate a device."

We can see how *authority* and *power* are often used interchangeably, but the clear difference between the two is that *power* is about having the capacity to influence or control something or someone. *Authority* is about having the right or permission to assert that power. The Bible clearly shows us that we have both the power and the authority to live full and victorious lives through Christ and to secure that fullness and victory for the generations that will come after us.

In Matthew 28:18 Jesus says, "I have been given all authority in heaven and on earth." Then in Luke 10:19 He says He has given us authority. Therefore the same power and authority that God gave Jesus, Jesus has given to us. We now have official permission, the right to act in a specified way, the power to influence others, and the power or right to give orders and make decisions.

We have been given divine authority, and not just to manage our lives, but we have also received authority from Christ to overcome "all the power of the enemy" (Luke 10:19). Realize, however, that the "we" I speak of are those who, through the power of the Holy Spirit, believe God and have accepted His Son, Jesus Christ. We are the ones who are endued with this power from above.

DIVINE KEYS ARE SPIRITUAL WEAPONS

It is often noted that we are in a battle where secular humanism wages war against the Spirit. We need weapons of the Spirit to win. The Bible says:

> We use God's mighty weapons, not worldly weapons, to knock down the strongholds of human reasoning and to destroy false arguments [idols and other strongholds].
> —2 CORINTHIANS 10:4

> We are not fighting against flesh-and-blood enemies, but against evil rulers and authorities of the unseen world, against mighty powers in this dark world, and against evil spirits in the heavenly places.
> —EPHESIANS 6:12

Divine keys can be used as spiritual weapons. We too, as soldiers in the army of the Lord, can be used as weapons. We can also be used as spiritual keys in a metaphorical sense. One Sunday my pastor, Theo McNair Jr. of Believers' Bible Christian Church in Atlanta, said during his sermon, "I am a weapon [for God to use]." When he said that, light bulbs flashed on in my understanding. If I am a weapon, then I am also a key. Wow!

There is much to be explored when we examine the keys for living a good life, the life that has been secured for us by Jesus's sacrifice on the cross. Each chapter in this book reveals a divine key to unlocking the authority that will unleash our spiritual gifts and empower us to use them to their fullest potential. This book is a prophetic gift designed to empower and release more of God's gifts in the earth, but the nature of the prophetic is that it never shuts off. There is always one more word, one more lesson, and one more revelation. However, the Lord has led me to begin with the twenty-one divine keys outlined in this book.

As you read on, you will discover that there is a purpose for your life, and when you align the gifts and talents that are inherent within you with the will and purposes of God, your gifts can bring you tremendous rewards, both natural and spiritual. When you walk in God's grace and in obedience to Him, the blessings that flow when you use your gifts and talents will be boundless.

DIVINE KEYS SHAPED MY LIFE AND MY FAMILY

I was born into a special family—and so were you. Every family is special because every person is special to God. Your family may have unique "legacy trademarks" as mine does. Our King family legacy is threefold: God's love, faith, and civil rights. Because of this legacy, people with a strong sense of their own purpose often ask us how they too can live out the dreams God has placed in their hearts.

If you are reading this book, you may have similar stirrings. You already know you have spiritual gifts or a spiritual calling and purpose for your life, and you long to do more for God. You may be interested in discovering how to develop your gifts and abilities beyond their natural expressions into what they can be supernaturally.

There is power inside of you—power to heal, dispel darkness in our world, solve problems, and so much more. Even if you are at the pinnacle of success, you may be sensing that there is more. The twenty-one divine keys to living out your purpose that I present in this book are to inspire you to define the legacy God has ordained for you and your family. I will use memories and lessons from my own life as a member of the King family, but I will also share testimonies, examples, Scripture verses, and concepts that will reveal to you how to do all that the King of kings has planned for you and more.

This book is not a chronology of events—there's no chronological order here. It is not only about the King family values because our values are His values. So look at this book as a journey of discovery as you go from faith to faith and glory to glory, learning what it means to live a life in line with the divine will of God for you.

God has provided a way for us to grow beyond simply existing as His creations to becoming His children and receiving the keys to His house—the kingdom. If we can learn to use the keys to God's kingdom to unleash His power into our purposes and accomplish His will in our lives, we will have unlocked the secret to our greatest victories.

Submission and obedience to our Creator lead to mastery of the keys to the kingdom. Not only will effective application of these keys bring sustainable peace and joy to our journey, but they will have everlasting transformative results in the overall plan and purpose for our lives.

Through the years, God has used my life in many ways, sometimes with my awareness and permission, sometimes without. Since He is sovereign, I am grateful. I wish I had time to tell you about all those occasions, but I'll share just a few. By the grace and mercy of God, I have been blessed to be a mother; a grandmother; the director of Civil Rights for the Unborn through Priests for Life; a founding member of National Black Pro-Life Coalition, Restore the Dream, Defund Planned Parenthood, and the Open Housing Movement; a Georgia state legislator; a college professor for nineteen years; an author; an actress; a songwriter; a filmmaker; a worship leader; and so much more. Who said we can do only one thing in life? Can't we build tents and preach at the same time, as suggested by the life of the apostle Paul in Acts 18:1–4?

God has more for us than we can ask, think, or imagine. Just when we think we've seen or done it all, God has more. With this in mind I have prepared Scripture reflections, personal reflections, and prayers at the end of each chapter to help you embrace all that God has for you. The Scripture reflections provide the biblical basis for the keys discussed in each chapter. The personal reflections are open-ended questions that will help you dig deep into your spirit to hone in on what the Spirit of the Lord is speaking to your heart. And the prayers solidify your open heart that is ready to receive what the sovereign God has for the next leg of your journey. Throughout the book I've also highlighted some of the spiritual truths that have kept the King family legacy alive all these years. I pray they will bless you and your family.

As we embark on this journey together, I pray that you never grow weary of experiencing the new opportunities God brings into your life to express His glory. I also pray that this journal of testimonies blesses you and that you are able to be strategically and supernaturally moved along the path to unleashing your full potential in God.

SCRIPTURE REFLECTION

> They shall speak of the glory of Your kingdom, and talk of Your power, to make known to the sons of men His mighty acts, and the glorious majesty of His kingdom. Your kingdom is an everlasting kingdom, and Your dominion endures throughout all generations.
> —PSALM 145:11–13, NKJV

> Yours, O LORD, is the greatness and the power and the glory and the victory and the majesty, indeed everything that is in the heavens and the earth; Yours is the dominion, O

LORD, and You exalt Yourself as head over all. Both riches and honor come from You, and You rule over all, and in Your hand is power and might; and it lies in Your hand to make great and to strengthen everyone.

—1 CHRONICLES 29:11–12, NASB

PERSONAL REFLECTION

What physical keys do you possess? To what do they give you access? Are you still energized by what you can close, open, or operate? If not, what can you do to reshape your perspective on the things God has given you charge over? Is it time to do an inventory of your keys?

PRAYER

Father God, thank You for Your Word and for the gifts and callings You bestow on us. Let us honor that which You have freely given to us by worshipping and obeying You in offering and expressing to You our love and gratitude and returning to You the firstfruits in and of our lives. As we pray to bind the forces of darkness and loose the power of heaven, may our gifts be unleashed to fulfill our purpose in life for Your glory. We pray this in Jesus's name, by the power of Your Holy Spirit. Amen.

King Family Ties

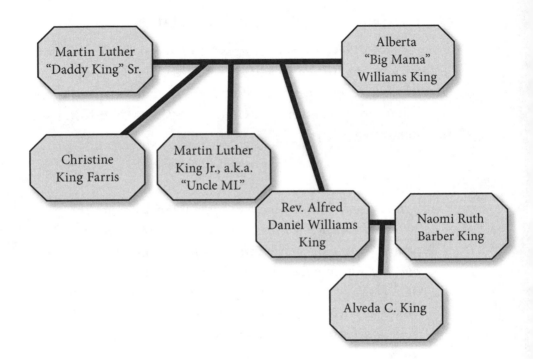

Next to me is my father, Rev. A. D. King, who set an example of faith, love, and service that I still seek to follow today.

Shown here are my father (right) and my uncle Martin Luther King Jr., who both gave their lives during the civil rights movement.

Chapter 1

DIVINE LOVE— THE MASTER KEY

We know how much God loves us, and we have put
our trust in his love. God is love, and all who live
in love live in God, and God lives in them.

1 JOHN 4:16

Y UNCLE MARTIN Luther King Jr. was often referred to as "the Black Moses" because he was recognized as a twentieth-century liberator. A lesser-known—yet equally, if not more, powerful—role he played was as a modern-day apostle of love.

In the Bible, John the revelator is recognized as a living example of Christ's love. Thousands of years later Uncle ML's message was patterned after the truth of the love of Jesus—and the whole world remains inspired to make changes in how they treat one another as fellow human beings.

Of all the divine keys we need to fulfill the purpose God has ordained for us, the most important one is love. It is the master key that unlocks every door. Love is the foundation and anchor of happiness and heightened success. It is the force behind the sanctity of life and regard for monogamous marriage between one man and one woman, which are divine keys I'll discuss in later chapters. Even mighty mountain-moving faith is fully revealed, expressed, and released by love.

Love can mean many things to many people, but the kind of love I am talking about comes from the Greek word *agapē*, which means "affection, good will, love, benevolence, brotherly love."[1] There are other kinds of love that we may be familiar with from the Greek language. One is *eros*, which is romantic love often shared between a husband and wife. This kind of love gets a lot of attention in books, movies, and chart-topping songs, but it is not the kind of love we receive from God. *Eros* is not unconditional but is based on emotions and can be temporary.[2] Agape love, on the other hand, is boundless, endless, and limitless—so much so that we could write volumes about and take ages to describe this type of unconditional love. This is the way God loves.

Love is the key that unlocks every door because God is love. Only by trusting in God can we fully experience the freedom and liberty that His love brings. It is His love that causes us to grow and prosper, and it is His agape love that we must demonstrate to others.

The Bible tells us, "For God so loved the world, that he gave his only begotten Son, that whosoever believeth in him should not perish, but have everlasting life" (John 3:16, KJV). Through His death and resurrection Jesus gave us a new and lasting commission, which is the greatest commission of all—to love unconditionally.

My family and the church community I grew up in recognized agape love as the most powerful force in the universe, and I grew up with love notes abounding in my life. In the family room of my paternal grandparents' home, my grandmother Alberta Williams King, also known as "Big Mama," hung a plaque we saw every time we went in to eat a family meal that read: "Love your enemies. It will drive them crazy."

KING FAMILY TRUTH

"Love your enemies. It will drive them crazy."
—Unknown

As I am writing this chapter, the Spirit of the Lord is prompting me to remind you that we are threefold beings—spirit, soul, and body. It is with the heart that we believe, love, and forgive. Our hearts, not our minds, are the epicenters of our beings; therefore we must receive God's agape love and let it unblock the arteries of our spirits, souls, and bodies so we may live long and prosper on the earth.

EXPRESSIONS OF AGAPE LOVE INSPIRE US

I believe there are some secular love songs that were intended to be worship songs. I am thinking of the song "I Will Always Love You." With lyrics that will tug at your heartstrings, the song was written in 1973 and originally recorded by American singer-songwriter Dolly Parton. Whitney Houston recorded a version of the song for her 1992 movie, *The Bodyguard*. The song was also covered by artists such as Linda Ronstadt and John Doe.

What makes this song a classic is its powerful theme of an undying love. With minor transformation, Dolly's song could easily have been made to express our undying love for God. And while it was intended to be a song of parting, we have the promise that Jesus will never leave us or forsake us. Knowing Christ's love, sacrifice, and eternal promises can take our understanding of agape love to a new level.

KING FAMILY TRUTH

"I have decided to stick with love. Hate is too great a burden to bear."[3]

—Martin Luther King Jr.

My understanding of the love of God grew tremendously when I became a member of Believers' Bible Christian Church in Atlanta. The founding pastor, T. Allen McNair Sr., was a spiritual mentor to me. A lot of what helped me live out the King family legacy came from his teachings and revelations, and you'll get to experience some of them as well as I recall them throughout the various keys in this book.

During his lifetime Pastor McNair often taught of the power of love based on 1 Corinthians 13:8: "Love never fails" (NIV). It was his teaching on the revelation of God's love that helped me understand that love is the key that unlocks every door. What I will share in the remainder of this chapter is drawn from his teachings on the love of God. I pray it blesses you as much as it has blessed me.

T. Allen McNair Sr. is the late senior pastor and cofounder of Believers' Bible Christian Church in Atlanta, Georgia.

REVELATION OF THE LOVE OF GOD

When we as believers come to know the love of God personally, nothing will stop us. All problems of human suffering that we experience can be addressed with the agape love of God. Stumbling blocks become building blocks when we apply agape love to any situation. "Build your hope on things eternal, hold to God's unchanging hand" are the words of a popular Christian song.[4] Our hopes for a better life become reality when we apply faith, which works by love (Gal. 5:6).

Today we live in a fast-paced world where material possessions are often more valuable to us than kind and loving relationships. Why? For some it is easier to acquire material gain than it is to express genuine agape love. Meanwhile, family relationships are being starved to death. People try to feed one another by portraying Hollywood personas, with all the fancy hair, clothes, cars, and such. And simple acts of compassion and human kindness become a pretense that they show to the outside world and drop on the doorstep when they get home.

People suffer enough at work, at school, and out in the cold, cruel world. When we get home, we should be prepared to give kind words, actions, and thoughts toward those who are closest to us. Notice that I say *give*, not *get* and not *receive* from others.

How often do we say, "I will love him or her when he or she gives me some love"? Yet in order to get love, you have to give love. That's in line with the law of sowing and reaping. If you sow much, you reap much. If you sow little, you get little. (See 2 Corinthians 9:6.)

Oh, how easy it is to put on displays of love that look good in public. At church, when it's time to greet our neighbor, we put on the biggest show of smiling and hugging. Yet sometimes before we reach the parking lot after service, we are ready to give someone a piece of our mind, not realizing that a mind is a terrible thing to waste. We need to have our whole minds, and added to that, the mind of Christ and the love of God—for God is love, and "love covers a multitude of sins" (1 Pet. 4:8, NIV).

John, love's apostle

Often when counseling people, I advise them to read the Book of 1 John. This little book teaches us more about love than we could ever learn from love songs on the radio or from popular books and movies. John, often called "the Revelator," is also known as "the apostle of love." He wrote several books in the Bible, including the Gospel of John; First, Second, and Third John; and the Book of Revelation. History reports that John was so well developed in a life of agape that he couldn't be killed. Reportedly, after surviving a sentence of being boiled in oil, he was exiled to the island of Patmos, where he wrote the Book of Revelation.

In order to model the kind of love John exemplified, we need a revelation. The revelation of the love of God is wrapped up in the reality of the Lordship of Jesus Christ. It is not about being kind, although being kind comes along with God's love. It is not about being emotional. The love of God was revealed to the apostle John, and God will reveal His love to you!

You will have to go deep to find it. The Bible says to seek the Lord with all your heart (Jer. 29:13). The Word also says to love the Lord with your entire mind, your heart, your soul, and your strength (Luke 10:27). Can you truly say you are doing this today? Do you really want to see the love of God manifested in your life? If so, you need to love God with all of your being and love other people as you love yourself (Mark 12:30–31). Jesus said these are the most important commandments.

Love manifested and dwelled among us

In the Gospels of Matthew, Luke, and John we see where Jesus first met John. James and John were fishermen with Peter. John caught the greatest revelation of the love of God during his walk with Jesus. The life Jesus lived—never changing, no matter what anyone did or said to Him—affected John. John decided to live with this reality in his own life. In the Book of John, chapter 1, John wrote: "In the beginning was the Word, and the Word was with God, and the Word was God" (v. 1, NKJV).

John was saying that Jesus and what He says are the same. What He says will never pass away. He is still upholding all things by the power of His word. Jesus's relationship with God is so much more than just His being born of a virgin. His relationship with God was revealed in how He dwelled among us.

Miracles such as turning water to wine must have been awesome. How would you feel having lived with someone who raised people from the dead? Someone who walked on water? Caused demons to depart? The demons recognized Jesus. Realize now that John had the awesome experience of knowing Jesus—really knowing Him. It was not a religious experience; it was a real one.

There is something in the Book of First John that will affect your life. In the life and testimony of John, God is giving us the revelation of Jesus. Here was a man who was also God who defied the powers of that age. The Pharisees and the government couldn't contain Him. Yet who can contain the love of God? Only those who believe.

There was no question in John's mind that heaven exists and the devil is real. People debate these issues today because they do not have the revelation John had. John knew that when Jesus said, "Roll the stone away," a miracle would occur. John knew that He who set time into existence could call Lazarus forth. John left us the road map in his first letter: "That which was from the beginning, which we have heard, which we have seen with our eyes, which we have looked upon, and our hands have handled, concerning the Word of life" (1 John 1:1, NKJV).

Yes, John knew that he had witnessed the embodiment of the love of God and the living Word of God: "The life was manifested, and we have seen, and bear witness, and declare to you that eternal life which was with the Father and was manifested to us" (1 John 1:2, NKJV).

A heart to receive

Yes, the love of God can be manifested if you have the heart to receive it! John did. Do you? He wrote: "That which we have seen and heard we declare to you, that you also may have fellowship with us; and truly our fellowship is with the Father and with His Son Jesus Christ. And these things we write to you that your joy may be full" (1 John 1:3–4, NKJV).

Is your joy full today? If so, glory be to God. Pass it on. If not, keep pressing on. This love is available to you. This is not just a religious saying. This is not a storybook tale. You can know the love of God!

John had a face-to-face encounter with the love of God. Jesus looked like a man, but He was so much more outstanding. John was allowed to go on the Mount of Transfiguration with Jesus. After that experience John was even more convinced that Jesus could accomplish whatever He set out to do. John understood that Jesus controlled the armies of the world. John understood that all power belonged to Christ. John said he'd looked upon Him and handled the words of life!

Here was a being in a physical body, yet John knew that he'd had the occasion to touch the One who had framed the worlds and all creation. John spoke from experience. He witnessed the Son of God free a woman bent with infirmity for eighteen years. John saw Jesus speak to the circumstances and saw the woman's body completely restored. Would you say that woman's joy was full after that?

This eternal reality became such a part of John that the Romans couldn't kill him. History tells us John lived through being boiled in oil. What a revelation of the power of the love of God!

Live in the abundant life of love.

Jesus said, "I have come that they may have life, and that they may have it more abundantly" (John 10:10, NKJV). Man did not have abundant life. He'd lost it when he was cast out of the Garden of Eden. Jesus brought it all back to us. Think about it. God told Adam that once he'd partaken of that tree, he'd surely die. God was saying a lot when He spoke those words. Then, hundreds of years later, after witnessing all kinds of deaths and curses, John lived to see love in action. John saw love alive. John touched and handled the love of God—and so can you! Can you handle it? More importantly, do you want to handle it? Do you want to touch and feel the Jesus whom John knew?

You must be aware that you don't have to be denomination minded. You don't have to be church minded! You don't have to be church-duty minded. When you receive a revelation to serve God with all your heart, mind, and soul—serving the eternal, everlasting Word of God, who is just as real today as He was two thousand years ago—then you are on the road to living the love that John knew.

Learn the way of love.

Many of us understand mathematics, English, or science because we have applied ourselves to learn those subjects. When someone wants to master a topic, he will study it. Often athletes will major in sports, and singers will major in voice because they want to become excellent in those arenas. But too many Christians don't apply the same principle to learning their faith. When we study topics with an intent of mastering them, we do just that. But when we are lackadaisical in our efforts to learn something, the opposite happens, even in spiritual matters.

We Christians are failing when it comes to spiritual things. In our knowledge and application of spiritual truths, we don't even know two plus two equals four. If the church were a learning institution (which it should be), most Christians would be making failing grades. We get after kids for playing hooky, yet we play spiritual hooky all the time. The "professor" (the Holy Spirit) is in class, but the students don't show up.

The things we should know most of all, we know least of all. The spiritual things that directly affect our lives, we don't know. We are not like John. We've not had the spiritual experience of handling the Word of life. We want to treat the preachers like doctors. We don't have to know what they know to get well. We don't have to know how to use the tools the doctor uses. We expect the doctor to know what will help us get well. Yet the Bible says people perish for lack of knowledge (Hosea 4:6).

We need the knowledge the Word is giving us. We need to understand healing, prosperity, and whether we are in right standing with God. We need to know the assistance we have from angelic forces. But so many of us don't know these things, so life remains a mystery to us. We fail to comprehend spiritual things. And many times we won't try to.

Until we come face-to-face with the reality that we must know God's love personally, our experience will always be surface level and secondhand. It will almost be like trying to get somebody else to breathe for us or to get his or her heart to beat for ours. It won't work. We have to touch, know, and handle this reality for ourselves. We must personally know our God.

The Word of God should be just as real in our everyday lives as the Bible that we open up and read is. We need to pray and ask God to reveal His Word to us—and not just from a book but in our everyday realities. When we ask God to reveal His Word to us, we must allow Him to do it. Then we can live the Word and do the Word!

Make it real.

From Genesis 1 to the last page of Revelation the Word of God should be real to you. The fall and redemption of man should be just as real to you as breathing. You need to know that God is involved in your life. You are a product of the plan and purpose of God! His love is higher than anything else you can ever think of. You are a member of the family of God.

The issue of racial ties becomes irrelevant with the revelation that according to Acts 17:26, we are not separate races but rather one human race. Also, it is important to remember that while our God-ordained ethnic distinctions remain relevant, they should never divide us.

Racial disputes, social differences, and a lack of associations should not separate us. Being members of God's family should bring us together. Unfortunately this hasn't happened because there isn't a full revelation of the love of God in the church. When you're more focused on yourself than on God, you don't have a revelation of God. When you're looking at yourself and the differences in other people, you're not seeing God, the Father, Son, and Holy Spirit. To have a revelation of God is to have a revelation of the love of God.

This should be a reality in your life that grows more and more every hour, day, and year. There should be a depth in your understanding and application of this love that wasn't there last year. Your purpose is to be fulfilled in the love of God, and you might want to start by majoring in 1 John. Once you get a handle on that, you can go on to learn the character of love in 1 Corinthians 13. Don't jump ahead of yourself, thinking you know it all when you don't have two plus two down. Touch, handle, and know the love of God bit by bit and firsthand.

"And now abide faith, hope, love, these three; but the greatest of these is love" (1 Cor. 13:13, NKJV). Keep yourselves in the love of God so your joy may be full, complete, and ever overflowing.

There's no success, influence, prosperity, or platform worth having without a revelation of God's love for His children. How can we understand God's plan for our lives without having a revelation of how much He loves us—how much of a future and a hope He has planned for us? Anything we achieve in this life will not carry the full weight of purpose and destiny without a real understanding of God's love. We can't truly believe the best for others without understanding God's love for them. But we can ask God to reveal His love to us. He says we can call out to Him, and He will show us great and mighty things we don't know (Jer. 33:3). The great and mighty love of God is the master key of the kingdom that unlocks every other truth we are going to explore in this book. Each key is truly an expression of God's extravagant love.

SCRIPTURE REFLECTION

God is love.

—1 JOHN 4:8

PERSONAL REFLECTION

How would you describe God's agape love?

PRAYER

*Dear heavenly Father, teach me how to love, even as Christ loves You and through You loves me enough to have laid down His life for me and risen again after defeating our enemy the devil and forever becoming our High Priest. Your Word promises in 1 Corinthians 13:8 that "love never fails" (*NIV*). Thank You for Your unfailing love. In Jesus's name, amen.*

Chapter 2

DIVINE SALVATION

God saved you by his grace when you believed. And you can't take credit for this; it is a gift from God. Salvation is not a reward for the good things we have done, so none of us can boast about it.

—Ephesians 2:8–9

THERE IS A beautiful song written by Greg Nelson and Phil McHugh called "People Need the Lord." It was made popular by Christian singer Steve Green in 1984, and while many people have heard and love the song, not many know the testimony of the men who wrote it. Nelson shared the story in Lindsay Terry's book *I Could Sing of Your Love Forever*:

> We were trying to write a song one day and spent most of the morning talking about ideas. We decided, about lunchtime, to go to a restaurant near my office in Nashville. After we were seated, a waitress came to our table, and as she approached us she smiled. Yet it seemed that her eyes were so empty. She was trying to convey a cheery attitude, but her face seemed to say something else. She took our order and walked away.
>
> We looked at each other and one of us said, "She needs the Lord." We then began looking around the restaurant at all of the people. They, too, seemed to have an emptiness in their faces. We sensed a real heaviness in our hearts as we watched them.
>
> Suddenly we realized that all of those people needed the Lord. Just as quickly, we both thought: *We need to write that—people need the Lord*. We finished our meal and went back to my office and sat down to write what was in our hearts. The pictures from the restaurant that remained in our minds, coupled with the realization that millions of people around the world are also groping for some ray of light, gave rise to "People Need the Lord."[1]

My testimony was very much like that of the waitress and many of the customers in the restaurant. In 1983, just one year before "People Need the Lord" was released, I had been living life as a member of the famous Martin Luther King family. I was just thirty-two years old, yet I had experienced many worldly successes in my life. I was a stage and screen actress, had just completed two terms as a Georgia state legislator, had college degrees, was married to a wealthy physician, and was a mother of three children. The fact that I was post-abortive was one of the secret regrets I hid from the world with my smile and my big checkbook.

To the world I was a great success. In my soul I was secretly sad. But that changed in the fall of 1983 when I accepted a position as an associate professor in a local college in Atlanta. There, I was led to Christ by a colleague.

During my first weeks at the college I had been warned by other colleagues to "stay away from the Bible-thumping Christian." At the time, this woman carried with her all the time a large red binder with a cross embossed on the front.

Well, I must admit that I had a pretty rebellious spirit in those days. I was also a know-it-all. So I ignored the advice of the naysayers and approached this "Bible-thumper." I remember asking her why people thought I should avoid her. She answered my question with a question of her own: "Alveda, are you saved?"

Since I honestly didn't know what that meant, I asked her this: "Saved from what? Or whom?"

Then she asked me if I had accepted Jesus into my life. I told her how at the age of five I had received the right hand of fellowship into our church and how I was then allowed to take communion with the church members. I thought it was such an honor to drink that grape juice and eat that cracker back then.

Thinking back, I believed what the preachers administering the Communion elements were teaching: that Jesus had served the Last Supper to His disciples, had been crucified, and after three days had risen again. I just didn't get the part that Jesus died for my sins, because at the age of five I was clueless to the truth that I was a sinner.

As I was explaining all of this, and while she was still holding her Bible close to her heart, she stopped me in mid-sentence and asked, "Alveda, who is Jesus?"

I answered her with my best Sunday school theology. That wasn't good enough. She asked again, "Alveda, who is Jesus?"

This time my pride and arrogance answered her. I rapped off quickly, "He was born of the Virgin Mary, died, and rose again." Why, I almost sang that Sunday school ditty "He 'rose, He 'rose, He 'rose from the dead…"

My agitation didn't deter her. She asked a third time, "Alveda, who is Jesus?"

Well, I'd had just about enough then and was about to give her a piece of my mind. I put my hand on my hip and whirled around to face her, and just as I was about to let her have it, God let me have it. The lights came on. It was like a real flash of light. I dropped my hand from my hip, and my jaw dropped at about the same time. At first I mumbled so low that I wondered if she had heard me. I said, "I guess He's God." Then I took a step toward her and proclaimed with all my heart for the first time in my life, "Wait, I know He is God!"

It was on for sure then. With every question I asked her, she took me to a scripture for my answers. It was like the Queen of Sheba coming to prove King Solomon. I wanted her to prove that Jesus is the Son of God. She was surely an able vessel.

That day I realized that I had been attempting to worship and serve the God of my parents and grandparents, but now I was saved. I became hungry for God's Spirit and the truth of His Word. Pretty singing and fancy preaching were no longer good enough. I was hungry for the Word. I stopped attending our family church and began to visit Spirit-filled churches that I had seen and heard about on television. I was wondering if the miraculous healing I saw on evangelist Ernest Angley's television broadcasts was real. I wanted to know all about the "speaking in tongues" thing some people did.

KING FAMILY TRUTH

"By opening our lives to God in Christ, we become new creatures. This experience, which Jesus spoke of as the new birth, is essential if we are to be transformed nonconformists."[2]

—Martin Luther King Jr.

WELCOME, HOLY SPIRIT

One day I met a friend on the street, Mrs. Gerri Thompson. Now deceased, she was the wife of one of my earlier spiritual mentors, pastor Wayne Thompson, founder of Fellowship of Faith Church in Atlanta. Pastor Wayne is known by many in Atlanta as the granddaddy of faith. The thing is Pastor Wayne had been my boss when I was working my way through college a few years before. Back then, he certainly wasn't a preacher. Somehow along the way Wayne and Gerri had found the Lord and started a church.

Sister Gerri invited me to their church that day on the street. I was curious, so I took my little children with me to visit the church one Sunday. I sat in the back and joined in as the worship team and congregation sang songs I had heard by the Christian ministries I had been watching on TV. Then they began to sing in a language I didn't understand. I was mesmerized.

Since I knew many of the songs they were singing, I fit right in. I continued to sing along, and as I worshipped with the congregation, I found myself also singing in an unknown tongue. What a joy! I still sing in unknown tongues and in my own native English language today.

It was during this same season that my childhood friend prophetess Phyllis Norwood Fisher introduced me to the song "People Need the Lord." We had gotten saved around the same time and ended up attending the same church for that season. I remember weeping the first time I heard the song. It wasn't just a pretty song for me. It wasn't Christian entertainment. It was a lifeline. There is so much truth in the lyrics and a life-changing anointing in the melody.

WHO IS JESUS TO YOU?

It's interesting to consider what it can sometimes take to lead a person to the Lord. It can be a song or a prayer, a cataclysmic brush with death, or countless other promptings that light that spark that leads to salvation. Fueled by the Antichrist, issues such as genocide, infanticide, gendercide, abortion, euthanasia, and all manner of inhumanity to man have plagued nations and civilizations throughout the ages. Human rights questions, civil rights questions, and religious rights questions continue to divide the hearts of humanity.

But salvation through faith in Jesus Christ brings healing and justice to all these issues and more. Salvation is a divine key because we have no godly spiritual authority if we are not in Christ. We can't even begin to think about aligning with the King of kings without first being saved.

If you are not sure, as I wasn't sure, who Jesus really is in your life, I invite you to open your heart to Him. Ask Him to come into your heart today, pray for the Holy Spirit to come and fill you, and get connected in a strong Bible-believing church to help build a foundation for God to lay His blessing upon. As my uncle ML once said, "Man cannot save himself, for man is not the measure of all things and humanity is not God. Bound by the chains of his own sin and finiteness, man needs a Savior."[3]

SCRIPTURE REFLECTION

Don't you see how wonderfully kind, tolerant, and patient God is with you? Does this mean nothing to you? Can't you see that his kindness [goodness] is intended to turn you from your sin?

—ROMANS 2:4

The wages of sin is death; but the gift of God is eternal life.

—ROMANS 6:23, KJV

PERSONAL REFLECTION

God's goodness draws people to Him. Do you draw people to God or drive them away with harsh judgments and creepy cryptic warnings?

PRAYER

Lord, use me to shine Your light and love so people can see and be drawn to You. In Jesus's name and by the power of Your Holy Spirit I pray. Amen.

Chapter 3

DIVINE FORGIVENESS

But when you are praying, first forgive anyone you
are holding a grudge against, so that your Father
in heaven will forgive your sins, too.

—MARK 11:25

AFTER MY REBIRTH in Christ, in 1983, one of my very first exercises in faith was to learn to forgive my enemies and myself. Forgiving myself was hardest. Like many people, I had become well versed in hiding my sins, failures, and regrets. But after I was born again, God began leading me to repent of my own sins and forgive those who had sinned against me.

My uncle ML was often noted for saying we must learn to love God, others, and ourselves. Well, in my early faith and love walk I was quickly learning it is impossible to love someone while harboring angst against him or her.

KING FAMILY TRUTH

"Love is the key to the solution of the world's problems, yes, even love for enemies." [1]
—Martin Luther King Jr.

At Fellowship of Faith Church, my first church home after being born again, there were deliverance services where we received prayer to be freed of unforgiveness and other sins. At those services we were invited to write lists of people we were harboring bad feelings against and to forgive them.

The church also introduced me to the concept of debt collecting as the basis for justifying our grudges. In our unrepentant state we learned to refuse to forgive someone unless that person apologized to us. In other words, until we received the apology we demanded, we would not forgive our offenders. Instead, we would hold them in debt to us because we believed they owed us an apology.

In my new, born-again life it was absolutely a foreign concept that instead of people owing me an apology, I owed them forgiveness. Why? I owed others my love and forgiveness because Jesus had paid for my sins and God had forgiven me, so it was time for me to forgive others.

Mark 11:25 says, "But when you are praying, first forgive anyone you are holding a grudge against, so that your Father in heaven will forgive your sins, too." Allen McNair, my pastor for many years, often taught that our sick bodies correlate to our sick souls and weak spirits. As I was reflecting upon and then writing this chapter, this word came to me: Forgiveness heals your heart and unblocks your arteries.

Because we are spiritual creations who have souls and live in human bodies, we have both physical and spiritual aspects to our beings. Somehow our physical organs and bodily systems are connected to their soulish and spiritual counterparts. We have physical hearts that beat and pump our lifeblood. Then we have the hearts at the cores of our souls. I'm referring to that "man of the heart" that guides our wills, minds, and emotions.

Pastor Tim McNair, who is Pastor Allen McNair's son and a minister at BBCC, often teaches on the importance of forgiveness. He teaches how he has received healing in his spirit, his soul, and even his body by forgiving himself and others for real and imagined injuries sustained over the years. He says unforgiveness can block the arteries of our hearts, both the spiritual and the natural.

Thus we can begin to understand that as our physical systems can be unblocked by surgery and medication, our spiritual systems can be unblocked, unlocked, and healed by love, forgiveness, prayer, and all of heaven's divine spiritual keys.

Recently, during a Q&A after a presentation I gave on God's grace and forgiveness, someone asked me, "How do you learn to get past guilt and shame to forgive yourself?" In response to this question, I shared two personal examples of how unforgiveness in my life once caused pain and grief, not only for me but also for others in my world.

FORGIVING THE DEEP HURTS OF RACISM

The first example is how I had to overcome unforgiveness regarding racism that others and I experienced during the civil rights movement. It would be many years before I would come to understand the truth of a favorite scripture among the preachers in our family, Acts 17:26: "And hath made of one blood all nations of men for to dwell on all the face of the earth" (KJV). One blood, one human race—that's a Bible truth.

KING FAMILY TRUTH

"And hath made of one blood all nations of men for to dwell on all the face of the earth."
—Acts 17:26, KJV

In my earliest years growing up, from 1951 to 1958, I had very little awareness of racial bigotry, surprising as that might sound. I also had little knowledge that we were all part of God's one race and how this truth is at the heart of the beloved community our family preachers often spoke of in their sermons.

I was raised in a close, nurturing community, and my family members did as much as they could to insulate my siblings, cousins, and me from the brutality of racial segregation, which breeds the ravages of racism. We never ate at restaurants outside our neighborhood, and no one told me at the time that this was because so many places wouldn't serve us. Big Mama, my paternal grandmother, always made me go to the bathroom at home before outings; she didn't want to explain the "white" and "colored" signs hanging over restroom doors.

I didn't get a vivid, firsthand picture of racism until the 1960s after my parents moved us to Birmingham, Alabama, where Daddy had accepted the assignment to become pastor of First Baptist Church in Ensley. It was in Birmingham that Daddy took my brothers and me to our first civil rights protest—the Children's Crusade of 1963. The march took place in May, just months before the bombing of the 16th Street Baptist Church, where four little girls were killed, and about a week before our home was bombed on the eve of Mother's Day.

Often during those years, as we drove through some of the wealthier—and exclusively white—neighborhoods to see Christmas decorations, I would ask Daddy why we didn't live in communities that looked like those neighborhoods. After years of isolating my siblings and me from the ugly truth of segregation, Daddy began to explain to us the realities of racism.

Through the years there were family weddings, graduations, and milestone birthdays. There were also bombings, protests, and marches, including the historic March on Washington in 1963, where my uncle ML gave his famous "I Have a Dream" speech. We eventually moved from Birmingham to Louisville, Kentucky, where Daddy began the Kentucky Christian Leadership Conference (KCLC), which called for fair housing for all Americans. I was right beside him during the open housing marches, where we rallied for the right for all of us to live anywhere we could afford. It was there that I experienced my first arrest, which was—for me, at least—a badge of honor.

If these memories were to be the extent of my experience with racism, I would consider myself to have been truly fortunate. But you already know that racism exacted a horrible toll on my family, and for a time I nearly succumbed to the hatred that allows racism to fester.

On April 4, 1968, my uncle ML was assassinated. I was seventeen years old and was in the midst of the final fitting for my ROTC ball gown. The periwinkle blue dress was a princess cut with a flounce at the hemline and handcrafted rosettes around the neckline and hems. It's funny how details such as these become imprinted in our memories during times of joy or tragedy.

When the announcement of the shooting appeared on the TV screen, I was horrified. I quickly changed clothes, rushed out to my car—a gift from my precious daddy—and hurried home.

Daddy had just arrived home by private jet from Memphis, Tennessee, to comfort us before he was to fly back to Atlanta to escort Aunt Coretta back to Memphis to attend to the body of our beloved Martin Luther King Jr.—loving husband, father, brother, son, uncle, and so much more.

In our kitchen, standing by the back door to the breezeway to our garage, I was inconsolable. I was a young youth organizer in the civil rights movement. Uncle ML was a global leader and hero. Daddy was his brother, the president of the KCLC and a leader in the current fair-housing movement.

Our family had survived the bombing of our home, the incarcerations of Uncle ML and Daddy, brutal beatings, death threats, and so much more. We had been taught to love and forgive our enemies. But in that moment that was the last thing I wanted to do.

LETTING GO

Soon after Uncle ML was killed, I went away to college at Murray State in Kentucky. I had two roommates, one who was black and one who was white. One day the subject of race came up, and the emotions I'd been harboring came to the surface. I began to weep, and my white roommate tried to comfort me, but I rejected her. What did she know about the feelings of black people? "Get away from me!" I yelled. "I hate you—you killed my uncle!" So many times I have wished and prayed for just a moment to see her again, to ask her to forgive me, to apologize for those misguided feelings and emotions.

Those were the same feelings my father tried to get me to let go of after Uncle ML was killed. Yet deep in my heart I was seething with contempt for the people I erroneously blamed for stealing him from us, judging them all based on the color of their skin.

"I hate white people," I had cried to my father over and over again as he held me in his arms, pleading for me to forgive those who had committed this deep harm, not just to our family but also to the world. "They killed my uncle," I insisted.

Daddy was always an extremely loving and patient man, and he maintained that patience even in the face of devastating grief. He also maintained his belief in the "Beloved Community," a philosophy my uncle articulated.[2] He told me, "White people didn't kill your uncle, Alveda. That was the devil." He refused to allow me to hate, and he reminded me of his unfailing belief in our mutuality. That he was able to offer this example when he'd just lost the brother he loved so very much was a lesson I will never allow myself to forget. I'm just glad Daddy didn't give up and that he kept teaching me to love and forgive until the day he died, which came much too soon. He was killed just a year after Uncle ML's assassination.

Forgiveness didn't come cheap, nor was it ever easy for us. Not everybody in my family forgave those involved in the events that led to the deaths of Uncle ML and Daddy. Even I held on to the vestiges until I was born again in 1983.

Years after the deaths of his sons, Granddaddy (Daddy King) still carried an intense anger against some of the people who were with my uncle when he died. He held the greatest anger toward Jesse Jackson, who had been with my uncle—trying to convince Uncle ML in heated tones that nonviolence might no longer be the answer—when the shooting occurred. Daddy King believed it was Jackson's job to protect his son, and he wouldn't forgive Jackson for failing in that duty.

This conflict was finally resolved at the 1976 Democratic National Convention when Jimmy Carter received the presidential nomination. Daddy King was backstage in the wings, resting in a wheelchair, and as he prepared to go on the platform with the soon-to-be president Carter, someone told him that Jesse Jackson wanted to speak with him. Granddaddy bitterly refused, claiming Jackson was responsible for the death of his son.

Though I knew of his feelings for Jackson, I felt I couldn't let this pass. "Granddaddy, I don't understand," I said. "I thought you always told me that we can't hate anybody. Doesn't that mean Jesse Jackson too?"

Granddaddy looked at me with pain and confusion in his eyes. Finally, he nodded slowly and said, "You're right, girl." With that, he told the man who'd come to tell him of Jackson's request that he would be willing to see him. What I witnessed then was one of the most touching moments I've experienced in my life and one of the clearest indications of the power of love.

When Jesse Jackson came up to my grandfather, his face bore years of anguish and grief. He sat on Daddy King's lap, put his arms around his neck, and wailed, "I'm so sorry." Granddaddy was obviously moved by this declaration. "I forgive you," he said, and the two men at last got to mourn my uncle together. Everyone who witnessed it was changed by the event.

As I write this chapter, it has been more than four decades since that day at Jimmy Carter's nomination. In that time much has changed, including the fact that a man with brown skin has served two terms as president of the United States. Still, as much as we've accomplished, my uncle's vision of a Beloved Community remains in many ways unfulfilled.

The Beloved Community calls for us "to fight against poverty, discrimination, and violence in every form. And as human history unfolds, the forms that discrimination and violence take will evolve and change. Yet our commitment to overcome them must not change, and we must not shrink from the work of justice, no matter how unpopular it may become" or how satisfied some people might be with how far we've come.[3] Beyond our borders we need to stand with our brothers and sisters who are the victims of racial discrimination and so-called ethnic cleansing. As we are Americans, our message carries all over the world, and we must always raise our voices to cry out against injustice.

"We must all learn to live together as brothers," said Uncle ML—and I'll add *sisters* here—"or we will all perish together as fools."[4] We must one day unite and realize that we all come from the same Source, and it is more essential than ever that we realize we are all connected by our humanity.

KING FAMILY TRUTH

"We must all learn to live together as brothers [and sisters], or we will all perish together as fools."

—Martin Luther King Jr.

Once we the people of America—and indeed the whole world—acknowledge our commonality, oppression and bigotry can cease to exist in this nation and beyond, and freedom and unity can reach to the far corners of the world.

FORGIVING YOURSELF—RELEASING GUILT AND SHAME

In addition to releasing the hatred and bigotry I felt as a result of skin-color racism, I also had to forgive myself of my secret regret of having had abortions. For years I'd suffered the after-effects of abortions and other past sins, and the guilt and unforgiveness had left me sick and in bondage. I had to come to a point of forgiveness, which was very difficult for me to do. I believe it was harder for me to forgive myself than it was for me to forgive the doctors who aborted my children, the family members who either looked the other way or encouraged me to abort, and even society as a whole, which I would later blame for my decision to abort.

No matter what you're holding on to, forgiveness is the divine key to rid your life of shame, blame, and bitterness. When we truly repent and turn away from our sins, God forgives us. The Bible says in 1 John 1:9: "If we confess our sins to him, he is faithful and just to forgive us our sins and to cleanse us from all wickedness." So if God forgives us, then we must forgive ourselves as well as others who have hurt and offended us. During this process of forgiveness the healing begins. It's a painful process, to say the least, yet there is healing, grace, and light at the end of the tunnel.

GENUINE RECONCILIATION COMES WITH REPENTANCE

It is important to note that there can be no genuine reconciliation without repentance on both sides. There are always at least three sides to every situation. There is one person's side, the other person's side, and the unadulterated truth of the matter. In every case pride needs to be set aside so healing can come.

There is a very important scripture in James 3:14 that helps us clarify why there are human arguments and differences of opinion that often lead to hurt and unforgiveness: "But if ye have bitter envying and strife in your hearts, glory not, and lie not against the truth" (KJV). I like the way the verse reads in the New Living Translation: "But if you are bitterly jealous and there is selfish ambition in your heart, don't cover up the truth with boasting and lying."

In other words, don't say, "My way or no way. I'm right, and you are wrong. You don't agree with me, and that offends and hurts me, so I'm not going to hear you. But you must hear and agree with me." You cannot restore a relationship if you refuse to let go of pride.

During my lifetime I have had many opportunities to repent of striving against others and to love and forgive them instead. I've also had much to forgive of myself. When I chose to take those opportunities, I experienced true freedom. I invite you to think of how you may need to forgive others and yourself so you can experience the freedom and healing that repentance brings.

SCRIPTURE REFLECTION

> Then Jesus said to the disciples, "Have faith in God. I tell you the truth, you can say to this mountain, 'May you be lifted up and thrown into the sea,' and it will happen. But you must really believe it will happen and have no doubt in your heart. I tell you, you can pray for anything, and if you believe that you've received it, it will be yours. But when you are praying, first forgive anyone you are holding a grudge against, so that your Father in heaven will forgive your sins, too."
>
> —MARK 11:22–25

PERSONAL REFLECTION

Whom have you been holding in debt for not giving you an apology? Are you ready to ask God to help you release that person or those people, which will also set you free from the prison of unforgiveness? What do you need to forgive of yourself?

PRAYER

Heavenly Father, in the name of the Lord Jesus, I come. I confess my sins before You today and ask for Your forgiveness. Even as I ask for Your forgiveness, I ask You to help me forgive everyone who has sinned against me. I commend them to Your attention, grace, and mercy. I no longer hold anyone in debt to me, owing me an apology.

As I pray, I do confess and believe that Jesus is Your Son, was born of the Virgin Mary, lived and ministered on this earth for thirty-three years, died on the cross at Calvary, and shed His blood for my sins. He went into hell and defeated my enemy Satan and took the keys of hell and death. He rose again and went to heaven to sit on His throne on Your right hand and serve as my High Priest. He is coming back again soon, as He promised. He has given me the keys to Your kingdom and granted me Your authority to trample on snakes and scorpions and to overcome all the power of my enemy.

I believe this, Father, and ask You to take me as Your child, to deliver me from all sickness, disease, and every evil thing that has and could come against me. Break every yoke, Father. Fill me with Your Holy Spirit, and release Your ministering angels to take charge over me. Teach me, and lead me into my inheritance according to Your promise.

Thank You, Father. Praise You, Lord Jesus. Bless You, Holy Spirit. Father, I thank You for my liberty right now. I thank and praise and worship You right now! In Jesus's name, amen.

Chapter 4

DIVINE AUTHORITY

Behold, I give you the authority to trample on serpents
and scorpions, and over all the power of the enemy,
and nothing shall by any means hurt you.

—LUKE 10:19, NKJV

THIS BOOK DISCUSSES the application of our spiritual keys to unleash our spiritual gifts. Jesus appointed us to use the keys to God's kingdom (Matt. 16:19), and in order to use these divine keys and walk in our ministries, callings, and spiritual gifts, we must first understand them. The importance of understanding spiritual keys can be illustrated by one of my favorite memories.

As a little girl, I would gather with my siblings around Daddy when he came back from ministry trips he had been on either alone or with Uncle ML. He would sometimes have his monetary love offerings in a money bag. When he did, he sometimes would pour the money out on his bed and allow us to count it. This was so exciting, mostly because Daddy's gifts would often spill over into his buying gifts for us too. Daddy and most members of our King family have always been generous givers of tithes and offerings. As a result, we have received great blessings from God.

One of Granddaddy's favorite scriptures was, "I have been young, and now am old; yet have I not seen the righteous forsaken, nor his seed begging bread" (Ps. 37:25, KJV). We were always taught that tithing and giving are part of the righteous life of a Christian that brings about the fulfillment of promises like the one in this scripture.

As I would gaze in awe at the gifts the people gave my family elders while they were on the road, I didn't realize back then that God would have the same type of blessings ahead for me. After I became born-again, I came to understand that I would never have to covet such gifts. They are part of God's reward for faithful service. Much like with the Levites of the Bible, God uses gifts from the people to supply the needs of His servants. (See also Philippians 4:17–19.)

In my personal ministry and even in my occupation as a public speaker I receive many gifts from trip sponsors and their audiences while on the road. I have been given keys to cities, original paintings, inspirational journals and devotionals, books, jewelry, exotic and gourmet foods, and many other items. Receiving these types of gifts often reminds me of the days when I traveled with my father, my grandfather, and my aunt by marriage, Coretta Scott King.

I believe this perfectly illustrates the different mind-set we are to have as Christians. We don't serve God in order to get material gifts. That is the way of the world. It's the method of those who covet the things of the world. Just as there is sensual wisdom and godly wisdom, there is worldly authority and heavenly authority, as James 3:15 tells us: "This is not the wisdom that comes down from above, but is earthly, unspiritual, [and] demonic" (ESV).

AUTHORITY IS AN END-TIMES KEY

We need this godly wisdom and understanding now more than ever. Acts 2:17 speaks of a time when God will pour out His Spirit on all flesh and spiritual gifts will abound. The key of divine authority will coincide with this end-times Latter Rain movement.

As the salt and light in the earth, Christians must be equipped with *dunamis*—Holy Ghost power—to use the spiritual authority that has been given to us for this season. I first discovered the *Believer's Authority* teaching during my early days at BBCC when Pastor McNair invited his members to study this curriculum from the ministry of Kenneth Hagin. Because of these teachings I learned to walk in my Christian authority according to the promises of God.

Submission and authority work together with all the other divine keys, revealing how Christians ought to interact with one another. Knowing this, we must apply the key of divine authority in our daily lives. As we walk in our authority while remaining humbly submitted to God, the fruit of the Spirit, listed in Galatians 5:22–23, will be in full bloom in our lives.

I'll talk more in the divine submission chapter about the ways that authority and submission go hand in hand. But for now let me state that in the framework of hierarchical relationships every authority must humbly submit to the accountability of a higher authority, with the highest of all authorities being God. We see this truth in Hebrews 6:13 when God made a promise to Abraham: "Since there was no one greater to swear by, God took an oath in his own name."

As author and Southern Baptist seminary professor Mary Kassian notes in her blog "7 Misconceptions About Submission," in a community structure the biblical covenant perspective of authority is modeled as husbands act as authorities in their homes yet remain submitted to Christ. They fulfill their responsibility by loving their wives as Christ loves the church, which is a sacrificial love. Such an environment of love fosters Christlikeness and prevents abuse. Kassian writes that "a wife whose husband is abusive can appeal to higher authorities for intervention and protection. It is the responsibility of the authorities to protect and seek the good of all those under their care."[1]

Again, Kassian writes, "For example, along with submitting to her husband, a Christian wife also has the responsibility to be transparent, speak truth, confront sin, and challenge her husband to ever-increasing levels of holiness. As heirs together of the grace of life (1 Pet. 3:7), both husband and wife have the responsibility to love, encourage, and build one another up; and to interact with forbearance, kindness, and humility. Biblical authority and submission contribute to mutuality; they do not diminish or detract from it—it's both-and, not either-or."[2]

AUTHORITY SUBMITS TO AUTHORITY

Jesus Christ is the perfect example of a person of authority who chose to submit to authority. He told His disciples, "Whoever wants to be a leader among you must be your servant, and whoever wants to be first among you must be the slave of everyone else. For even the Son of Man came not to be served but to serve others and to give his life as a ransom for many" (Mark 10:43–45).

One of my favorite examples of the proper use of Christian authority is found in the testimony of the centurion in Matthew 8:5–13:

> When Jesus returned to Capernaum, a Roman officer came and pleaded with him, "Lord, my young servant lies in bed, paralyzed and in terrible pain."
>
> Jesus said, "I will come and heal him."
>
> But the officer said, "Lord, I am not worthy to have you come into my home. Just say the word from where you are, and my servant will be healed. I know this because I am under the authority of my superior officers, and I have authority over my soldiers. I only need to say, 'Go,' and they go, or 'Come,' and they come. And if I say to my slaves, 'Do this,' they do it."
>
> When Jesus heard this, he was amazed. Turning to those who were following him, he said, "I tell you the truth, I haven't seen faith like this in all Israel! And I tell you this, that many Gentiles will come from all over the world—from east and west—and sit down with Abraham, Isaac, and Jacob at the feast in the Kingdom of Heaven. But many Israelites—those for whom the Kingdom was prepared—will be thrown into outer darkness, where there will be weeping and gnashing of teeth."
>
> Then Jesus said to the Roman officer, "Go back home. Because you believed, it has happened."
>
> And the young servant was healed that same hour.

We see here that even a leader with much authority must exemplify humility and the ability to submit to a higher authority. Jesus Himself said, "I tell you the truth, the Son can do nothing by himself. He does only what he sees the Father doing. Whatever the Father does, the Son also does" (John 5:19). One who walks in divine authority must be submitted to the will of God on a daily basis. This includes properly applying all the divine keys.

SUBMITTING OUR NEEDS TO THE AUTHORITY OF GOD

As we become gifted with divine authority and continue to grow in the things of God, we look away from things of the world. We cease to worry about the things of the world, learning to trust God for our power and provision. The Word of God gives us the necessary guidance for this process. In Proverbs 3:5–12, we are given five directives:

1. "Trust in the LORD with all your heart; do not depend on your own understanding" (v. 5).

2. "Seek his will in all you do, and he will show you which path to take" (v. 6).

3. "Don't be impressed with your own wisdom. Instead, fear the LORD and turn away from evil. Then you will have healing for your body and strength for your bones" (vv. 7–8).

4. "Honor the LORD with your wealth and with the best part of everything you produce. Then he will fill your barns with grain, and your vats will over-flow with good wine" (vv. 9–10).

5. "My child, don't reject the LORD's discipline, and don't be upset when he corrects you. For the LORD

corrects those he loves, just as a father corrects a child in whom he delights" (vv. 11–12).

Jesus says in Luke 12:22–32 (ESV):

> Do not be anxious about your life, what you will eat, nor about your body, what you will put on. For life is more than food, and the body more than clothing. Consider the ravens: they neither sow nor reap, they have neither storehouse nor barn, and yet God feeds them. Of how much more value are you than the birds! And which of you by being anxious can add a single hour to his span of life? If then you are not able to do as small a thing as that, why are you anxious about the rest? Consider the lilies, how they grow: they neither toil nor spin, yet I tell you, even Solomon in all his glory was not arrayed like one of these. But if God so clothes the grass, which is alive in the field today, and tomorrow is thrown into the oven, how much more will he clothe you, O you of little faith! And do not seek what you are to eat and what you are to drink, nor be worried. For all the nations of the world seek after these things, and your Father knows that you need them. Instead, seek his kingdom, and these things will be added to you.
>
> Fear not, little flock, for it is your Father's good pleasure to give you the kingdom.

SUBMITTING TO WORLDLY AUTHORITY

When our human leaders forsake the ways and Word of God, we must learn to look beyond the authority of flesh to the authority of God. Even our governments are subject to the authority of God. Unjust rulers have their day in the sun, yet they too have to answer to God in the end.

In Romans 13 we are admonished to obey civil authorities. What is often misunderstood is that civil authorities are also subject to God's authority. They are all assigned as instruments of God, either to bless a nation or to warn and judge a nation. Sometimes God will temporarily allow an oppressive government to bring a nation to repentance. Even in such cases, as we see with Moses and Pharaoh, once a nation repents, God raises up deliverers in the seasons of oppression.

The apostle Paul wrote:

> Let every person be loyally subject to the governing (civil) authorities. For there is no authority except from God [by His permission, His sanction], and those that exist do so by God's appointment.
>
> Therefore he who resists and sets himself up against the authorities resists what God has appointed and arranged [in divine order]. And those who resist will bring down judgment upon themselves [receiving the penalty due them].
>
> For civil authorities are not a terror to [people of] good conduct, but to [those of] bad behavior. Would you have no dread of him who is in authority? Then do what is right and you will receive his approval and commendation.
>
> For he is God's servant for your good. But if you do wrong, [you should dread him and] be afraid, for he does not bear and wear the sword for nothing. He is God's servant to execute His wrath (punishment, vengeance) on the wrongdoer.
>
> Therefore one must be subject, not only to avoid God's wrath and escape punishment, but also as a matter of principle and for the sake of conscience.
>
> For this same reason you pay taxes, for [the civil authorities] are official servants under God, devoting themselves to attending to this very service.
>
> Render to all men their dues. [Pay] taxes to whom taxes are due, revenue to whom revenue is due, respect to whom respect is due, and honor to whom honor is due.
>
> Keep out of debt and owe no man anything, except to love one another; for he who loves his neighbor [who practices loving others] has fulfilled the Law [relating to one's fellowmen, meeting all its requirements].

The commandments, You shall not commit adultery, You shall not kill, You shall not steal, You shall not covet (have an evil desire), and any other commandment, are summed up in the single command, You shall love your neighbor as [you do] yourself.

Love does no wrong to one's neighbor [it never hurts anybody]. Therefore love meets all the requirements and is the fulfilling of the Law.

Besides this you know what [a critical] hour this is, how it is high time now for you to wake up out of your sleep (rouse to reality). For salvation (final deliverance) is nearer to us now than when we first believed (adhered to, trusted in, and relied on Christ, the Messiah).

The night is far gone and the day is almost here. Let us then drop (fling away) the works and deeds of darkness and put on the [full] armor of light."

—ROMANS 13:1–12, AMPC

KING FAMILY TRUTH

"If any earthly institution [or custom] conflicts with God's will, it is your Christian duty to take a stand against it. You must never allow the transitory, evanescent demands of man-made institutions to take precedence over the eternal demands of the Almighty God."[3]

—Martin Luther King Jr.

AUTHORITY AS A SPIRITUAL WEAPON

As we are directed in Romans 13:12 to put on the full armor of light, let us remain mindful that as people of divine authority, we have access to heaven's armory and weaponry. As we apply our authority to "trample on serpents and scorpions, and over all the power of the enemy," we use heaven's keys and weapons.

Again, the apostle Paul wrote in 2 Corinthians 10:4, "We use God's mighty weapons, not worldly weapons, to knock down the strongholds of human reasoning and to destroy false arguments." As he said in Ephesians 6:13–18, we have access to the full armor of God:

> Therefore, put on every piece of God's armor so you will be able to resist the enemy in the time of evil. Then after the battle you will still be standing firm. Stand your ground, putting on the belt of truth and the body armor of God's righteousness. For shoes, put on the peace that comes from the Good News so that you will be fully prepared. In addition to all of these, hold up the shield of faith to stop the fiery arrows of the devil. Put on salvation as your helmet, and take the sword of the Spirit, which is the word of God.
>
> Pray in the Spirit at all times and on every occasion. Stay alert and be persistent in your prayers for all believers everywhere.

SCRIPTURE REFLECTION

So Queen Esther, daughter of Abihail, along with Mordecai the Jew, wrote with full *authority* to confirm this second letter concerning Purim.
—ESTHER 9:29, NIV, EMPHASIS ADDED

"But I want you to know that the Son of Man has *authority* on earth to forgive sins." So he said to the paralyzed man, "Get up, take your mat and go home."
—MATTHEW 9:6, NIV, EMPHASIS ADDED

PERSONAL REFLECTION

Are you walking in your spiritual authority?

PRAYER

Heavenly Father, I thank You for the authority of the believer available to me as Your child. In Jesus's name, amen.

Chapter 5

DIVINE GRACE
AND MERCY

So let us come boldly to the throne of our gracious
God. There we will receive his *mercy*, and we will
find *grace* to help us when we need it most.

—HEBREWS 4.16, EMPHASIS ADDED

THE WORD *GRACE* appears in the King James Version of the Bible 159 times.[1] Because *grace* can be described as the "unmerited favour of God,"[2] grace is a very important key to unlocking the power and authority of God, which is needed in the life of a believer who desires to reach his or her full potential. The key of divine grace has a companion—mercy. Together they can unlock many doors God wants to open for you.

Grace and *mercy* are words we hear often at church, but we don't always truly know what they mean. An Oxford dictionary defines them this way:

- Grace: "The free and unmerited favour of God, as manifested in the salvation of sinners and the bestowal of blessings; a divinely given talent or blessing; the condition or fact of being favoured by someone; a period officially allowed for payment of a sum due or for compliance with a law or condition, especially an extended period granted as a special favour."[3]

- Mercy: "Compassion or forgiveness shown toward someone whom it is within one's [God's] power to punish or harm."[4]

Many people use the word *grace* to describe the beautiful appreciation we express to God at mealtime. How often have we said to our families around the dinner table, "Let's say grace"? Yet how often have we failed to consider what *saying grace* means? Such a prayer should always be an acknowledgment that it is only by the grace of God that we are living, breathing, and enjoying every meal, all benefits coming from a loving and gracious God. Too often we fail to acknowledge God's grace even while going through the religious motions we have been taught to engage in each day.

Yes, please say grace at mealtime. However, don't limit your acknowledgment of and appreciation for God's grace to mealtime. We should express gratitude for every breath we take. This sounds impossible, doesn't it? If we were to be forever grateful, we would be forever praying, wouldn't we? Could this be why the Bible teaches us to "pray without ceasing" (1 Thess. 5:17, KJV)? Only with God are all things possible!

In *My Utmost for His Highest* minister and author Oswald Chambers wrote that grace is the "overflowing favor of God" and that we can draw upon it as needed through prayer, no matter what situation we face. Chambers goes on to say, "One of the greatest proofs that you are drawing on the grace of God is that you can be totally humiliated before others without displaying even the slightest trace of anything but His grace."[5]

SEASONS OF GRACE AND MERCY

As we consider the definitions of *grace* and *mercy*, we must also consider that the seasons of grace and mercy can run out. Also, the gift of unmerited favor can be abused. People can live their whole lives and never realize that the grace and mercy of God are divine gifts that bring much benefit to believers' lives.

God's grace and mercy can be present in a life and experienced to a certain degree or measure. Yet if the believer is not conscious of what is available and operating in his or her affairs, then the divine key may never be fully turned to open the doors that wield maximum power in the believer's favor.

I have experienced God's grace and mercy in my own life so many times. I remember one particular incident in the fall of 1968, just a few months after the assassination of my uncle ML. I was in college, and my world seemed topsy-turvy. I had a school friend who had committed suicide because her family wanted to move out of town and take her away from her boyfriend—a modern-day Romeo and Juliet story. My own parents, AD and Naomi King, were planning to move back to Atlanta and take my younger siblings with them. They were returning to Atlanta because my granddaddy needed Daddy to take Uncle ML's place next to him as co-pastor of Ebenezer Baptist Church.

One night I was sitting on a bench under a tree with my boyfriend, and we were arguing about something. I can't remember what the fight was about; things were so out of order in the world, anything could set us off at any time. Before either of us could realize what we were doing, I was screaming and yelling at him, and he put his hands around my throat, yelling back and telling me to "just shut up." I remember feeling very warm, and then it seemed that I was floating away. My conscious awareness seemed to actually leave my body, and I floated away from the scene of him shaking my body and screaming, "Wake up! Wake up! Come back!"

I'm not sure how long it took, but for a while I kept floating up and away through the trees. I could see my body, and I could hear his voice from what seemed like a great distance away, yelling, "Come back!" Then I floated back into my body, and he was still shaking me. Then he was holding me. (Believe it or not, I remained in that relationship.)

My choices regarding relationships didn't get much better. By 1973 I had been married and divorced and had undergone two secret abortions and a miscarriage. I was at a low point in my life. I was living with the trauma of my uncle ML being shot and my daddy being discovered dead in our swimming pool. As if that weren't enough, in 1974 my paternal grandmother, Alberta Williams King, was shot while playing "The Lord's Prayer" on the organ on a Sunday morning.

Shortly after, I was dating a man my grandmother had warned me about before her death. I had also taken to going to nightclubs, drinking with friends, and then driving home alone. I didn't know it at the time, but God's grace and mercy were upon my life, preserving me despite the choices I was making.

On another occasion during this season in my life I was leaving my favorite "watering hole" and got into my car. My friends begged me not to drive home alone. Of course I ignored them. I remember saying something foolish like, "My car is like an old horse. It knows the way home." It was a rainy night in Georgia, and as I neared home, I heard a very loud thunder clap. There was a deluge of water pouring over the car, and a live electrical wire broke loose and fell across my car. I was still quite tipsy. I looked around and was about to reach for the door handle when I heard a voice say, straight out of Psalm 46:10, "Be still, and know that I am God!"

KING FAMILY TRUTH

Be still, and know He is God.

Well, I can tell you two things: I was instantly sober, and I instantly obeyed. I dropped my hand away from the door handle and just sat there in the car, listening to the thunder rolling and the rain pouring down and watching the lightning flash. I promise you, if that song "Never Alone" hadn't already been written that night, I could have written it myself.

I don't know how long I sat there in the car. There was such a peace in my soul as I obeyed the voice of God. Finally the storm rescue team was on the street where I had rolled to a stand-still. My car engine was still running. The crew approached the car, shining flashlights on my face. They pulled the live wire off the car and tapped on my window: "Hello, are you OK? Are you alive?" It seemed like a funny question because if I had been dead, I wouldn't have been able to answer, would I have been?

In both instances, with the out-of-body experience and the audible voice of God saving my life by the power of His Word, I experienced the grace and mercy of God. His mercy and grace are amazing.

DON'T FRUSTRATE THE GRACE OF GOD

During a Wednesday night Bible study at my church our first lady, Octavia McNair, taught on grace. Her main text was Galatians 2:21 (KJV):

> I do not frustrate the grace of God: for if righteousness come by the law, then Christ is dead in vain.

And her companion scripture was Ephesians 4:30 (KJV):

> And grieve not the holy Spirit of God, whereby ye are sealed unto the day of redemption.

Now, I have read these Scripture verses many times over the last thirty-plus years. Yet when Minister Octavia taught about frustrating the grace of God that night, using that Scripture passage as a foundation and sharing her many experiences with the manifestations of God's grace in her life, I began to hear with new ears and see with new eyes. Along with not quenching and grieving the Holy Spirit of God, I realized I needed to refrain from frustrating God's grace. Faith, hope, love, grace, goodness, and mercy—these, along with many others, are not only keys to God's kingdom, but they are also spiritual forces that are sent from God for our good.

As I looked back over the years at how God in His mercy has kept me by His grace, I had to repent for not trusting God and even for having done frustrating things when I should have been trusting. That revelation in Galatians 2:21 and a newfound understanding of God as Adonai, Boss, and Master have taken me to new heights.

Years later, after I had listened to my grandfather and changed my mind about having yet another abortion, I was married to the father of my second son. Get this: one live birth, two abortions, a miscarriage, and, by the grace of God, I was pregnant again. What I didn't know was that Granddaddy had also persuaded my mother, Naomi Ruth Barber King, not to abort me in 1950, after he had seen me in a dream three years before my birth.

He told Mother: "Neenie, you can't abort that baby. She's a little girl with bright skin and bright red hair, and she's going to bless many people." Talk about "I have a dream"! Granddaddy had a dream, and here I am!

Granddaddy used that vision to persuade my mother to let me live, and it became a family secret. Daddy and Mother were married and had five children. Then, years later, I was about to abort my son. Granddaddy was still on the battlefield. I mentioned to him that I was on the way to Planned Parenthood for an abortion, and he said: "Alveda, you can't abort that baby. He's my great-grandson." The baby's father agreed with Granddaddy. We were married and had five children together. So today, by the grace and mercy of God, I am the mother of six living children, and I am a blessed grandmother as well. God's grace and mercy are amazing!

Years after all this, having been born again in 1983, I had adopted the practice of praying regularly over my children. One night when my daughter was in college and living on campus, I woke up well after midnight and began praying and interceding for her. The phone rang at about 2:00 a.m., and she said, "Mama, are you praying for me?"

Sitting there on the side of my bed, I answered, "Yes, I am praying."

She whispered into the phone, "Please stop. I can't have any fun."

I remember chuckling, lying back on my pillow, whispering, "Thank You, Lord," and going back to sleep.

AMAZING GRACE

I believe it was around that season that I began listening to Wintley Phipps' rendition of "Amazing Grace." Phipps is a world-renowned vocalist, education activist, motivational speaker, pastor, and founder of the US Dream Academy. In his role as a vocalist he has recorded many songs, but his rendition of "Amazing Grace" recorded at Carnegie Hall may be the most powerful performance of that song. He had this to say about that classic hymn:

> A lot of people don't realize that just about all Negro spirituals are written on the black notes of the piano....Probably the most famous...on this slave scale was written by...John Newton, who...used to be the captain of a slave ship and many believe [he] heard this melody that sounds very much like a West African sorrow chant. And it has a haunting, haunting plaintive quality to it that reaches past your arrogance, past your pride, and it speaks to that part of you that's in bondage, and we feel it. We feel it. It's just one of the most amazing melodies in all of human history.[6]

Pastor Phipps teaches about grace around the world, but he delivers tangible evidence of God's grace through his US Dream Academy. The mentoring ministry for at-risk youths was born after he got involved with a prison ministry, which opened his eyes to the high number of young African American men who were incarcerated. Sadly many of the young people who end up in prison are the children of inmates. He wanted to break the cycle of intergenerational incarceration, and his Dream Academy has become a vehicle of God's grace to that end.[7] Through it he empowers youths from high-crime and high-poverty communities to believe they can succeed in life and prepares them to realize their dreams.

He said, "One of the most exciting things that can ever happen in a child's life is to know that, 'You mean God thinks about me? Or God dreams about me? And he's got a dream for my life?' And when you catch a little glimpse of what that dream is, wow, it changes everything."[8]

We see in this beautiful testimony the nature of God's grace and mercy—His unmerited favor, which can touch the heart of any and every human being, meeting us at our point of need when we are at our weakest. Oh, if we can only be like the little children of the world, going past "amazing grace" just being the lyrics and melody of a pretty song to finding awe in the grace of God and having our hearts become filled with the knowledge of Him. Then we would be well on our way to being blessed by this divine key called grace.

> Amazing grace! how sweet the sound,
>   That saved a wretch; like me!
> I once was lost, but now am found,
>   Was blind, but now I see.
>
> 'Twas grace that taught my heart to fear,
>   And grace my fears relieved;
> How precious did that grace appear
>   The hour I first believed!
>
> The Lord hath promised good to me,
>   His word my hope secures;
> He will my shield and portion be
>   As long as life endures.
> When we've been there ten thousand years,   Bright
>   shining as the sun,

We've no less days to sing God's praise
Than when we first begun.[9]

SCRIPTURE REFLECTION

And he said unto me, My grace is sufficient for thee: for my strength is made perfect in weakness. Most gladly therefore will I rather glory in my infirmities, that the power of Christ may rest upon me.

—2 CORINTHIANS 12:9, KJV

For by grace are ye saved through faith; and that not of yourselves: it is the gift of God.

—EPHESIANS 2:8–9, KJV

For sin shall not have dominion over you: for ye are not under the law, but under grace.

—ROMANS 6:14, KJV

And if by grace, then is it no more of works: otherwise grace is no more grace. But if it be of works, then it is no more grace: otherwise work is no more work.

—ROMANS 11:6

PERSONAL REFLECTION

How have God's grace and mercy touched your life?

PRAYER

Heavenly Father, thank You for Your grace and mercy in my life. Please teach me to know when Your grace is near me, working for, in, and through me. Teach me to acknowledge Your grace and to thank and praise You for it. In Jesus's name I pray. Amen.

Chapter 6

DIVINE FAITH

With God all things are possible.

—MARK 10:27, KJV

I GREW UP IN the church, and many people in my family, myself included, are or were gospel preachers. For all of us the time came when we had to cut the umbilical cord, as it were, and grow up into a life with God for ourselves. For me this meant leaving my "family church," Ebenezer Baptist Church. For over a quarter of a century now I have grown in spirit and in truth at Believers' Bible Christian Church in Atlanta. During my early years there my pastor, Allen McNair, helped me understand the key of divine faith.

God gives us many blessings in life. Among the countless blessings I have received in my life on earth are the lessons learned from my four favorite mentors. Three of them are elders from my bloodline. From them I learned to receive God's miracles, to have a compassionate heart, and that love never fails.

My father taught me to believe in and later to experience the miracles of God. When I was a little girl, I would sit in the pews of churches where Daddy preached and listen to his sermons on the miracles of Jesus. When Daddy preached on the miracles of Jesus, I actually believed Jesus walked on water, turned water to wine, rebuked the winds and waves, multiplied the fish and loaves, healed the sick, and raised the dead.

When Granddaddy preached about how we must have faith, hope, and love and that we needed the compassion of God for the prisoners, sick, elderly, widows, and children, my heart went out to "the least of these."

When Uncle ML preached about the love of God, my heart learned to know God as my loving Father.

Uncle ML and Daddy had faith in the American dream, but more importantly they had faith in God. It turns out that Mark 11:22, "Have faith in God," has become one of my favorite scriptures. My grandfather, Martin Luther King Sr.; my daddy; Uncle

ML; and my spiritual mentor for twenty-eight years, Pastor T. Allen McNair, were all great men of faith. While they were here, they taught and exemplified faith in God. They showed me that through Christ all things are possible, if we only believe.

KING FAMILY TRUTH

Through Christ all things are possible, if we only believe.

I miss them all so very much. They were my family, my protectors, my heroes, my mentors, and my first Bible teachers, who helped me develop the authority I needed to access the key of divine faith.

LESSONS IN FAITH

Pastor McNair and his wife, Anna McNair, are the parents of three adult children, who now make up the leadership team of the church. Pastor McNair's son, Theo Jr. (or Pastor Teddy), now the lead pastor, once said: "Wishing and hoping will not bring you to your destination. Stimulate your faith. In order for you to arrive at a place you have not been, you must do something you've not yet done. You must trust God to give you the wisdom to apply [use] what you already have, to increase your ability [and gifts]."[1]

It is a blessing to see the "legacy of faith" continuing in our church as Pastor Teddy proves himself to be a great faith teacher like his father. For twenty-eight years my faith grew under the word of faith Pastor McNair Sr. taught us. I remember the first Faith Clinic I attended. It was sometime around 1990. One of the foundational scriptures for our curriculum was from Hebrews 11:1: "Now [right now!] faith is the substance of things hoped for, the evidence of things not [yet] seen [with human senses]" (KJV). That was something new for me back then. I had "seen" the faith of my family members in action. In many ways, out of love and respect, I emulated them. Yet there was no way for me to truly own their faith. I would have to develop my own.

But how could I learn to use my faith without having a Bible teacher? After being born again in 1983, I quickly understood that it would be impossible for me to please God without faith, so I began my quest to grow in faith. Under the teaching of Pastor McNair I was like a Mary learning at the feet of the Master; I was like Elisha to Elijah. I was like Timothy to Paul. I was a student; Pastor McNair was God's ordained teacher to our church body.

Through the years, I have come to learn that it is faith working by love that drives out the darkness and enables us to see the gifts God has given us unleashed for the purpose of glorifying God in the earth. Hence, by combining the agape love legacy from my King family roots with the foundational faith teachings of Pastor Allen McNair, I have practiced what I have been taught, and as a result I have grown to be the faith teacher and mentor God designed me to be.

I learned so many things about faith from Pastor McNair, both through his Sunday sermons and through his special classes. It would take at least a book to chronicle even just a few of them, but I want to share two truths that have helped me grow in faith.

Follow quickly, even if you don't understand.

In the Book of Genesis, God told Abraham (who was called Abram at the time) to pack up and leave his home and country and go to a strange land. Some of us might have questioned God, but Abraham obeyed, and his obedience counted as faith and righteousness in God's eyes (Heb. 11:8).

Sometimes God instructs us to do things that don't make sense to our natural minds, but we must be like Abraham and follow Him quickly. Thankfully God's commands will almost always be combined with the abilities He has given us. But if we don't have the natural and spiritual commitment at the time the instructions are given, there may be a period of preparation as we receive and perfect the gifts and abilities that will enable us to fulfill the call.

However, we must not begin to overthink and question how we will do what God is calling us to do. If we do, we can find ourselves stepping out of faith and over into doubt. Fear can be the detriment to God's will for our lives; we can reason ourselves out of following the paths God wants us to take.

Inquire of the Lord.

After Moses died, God called his assistant Joshua to lead the people of Israel into the Promised Land. As you can imagine, Joshua felt overwhelmed by the task, which is why God told him, "Be strong and courageous! Do not be afraid or discouraged. For the LORD your God is with you wherever you go" (Josh. 1:9).

Through Joshua's example we can learn how to follow God's will: receive a call, be trained, act out of wisdom and preparation, pray (inquire of the Lord), and always seek God's will. And when problems come, confront them head-on. The result: success!

I must stress here that as he stepped out in faith to follow God's call, Joshua inquired of the Lord. Every good idea isn't a God idea. Even when we know we're called, we have to pray to get the plan of God downloaded into our beings in order to successfully accomplish His will for our lives.

As we learn obedience and faith, we are being groomed not only to receive God's gifts into our lives but to be vessels of honor.

HOW GOD USED A CUP TO INCREASE MY FAITH

As I mentioned previously, one of my favorite verses is Mark 11:22, "Have faith in God." It's my favorite in part because I know firsthand how powerful this divine key of faith is.

When I first started attending what is now BBCC in 1988, I had no idea what was in store for me. I was still married to the millionaire doctor, living in the mansion downtown, driving the best cars, and teaching at the college. I was the mother of six living children, with the youngest at my breast, two in my arms, two teenagers, and one young adult. I just can't tell you how blessed this time was!

But my life would change dramatically. In 1992, while I was enrolled in the church's school of ministry, God allowed a series of what I considered at the time to be unfortunate events to alter the course of my life. Let me be very clear: I was born again, and I went through some seriously hard times. The consequences of my pre-born-again choices were still pursuing me. I was a "new creation in Christ," but I was still a babe in Christ with a lot to learn.

By Christmas of 1992 I was separated from my husband and facing foreclosure and the threat of having my utilities cut off. I had little or no food in the cabinets and no presents for my family and friends. I was still active in my new church home and paying my tithes and offerings (against the advice of naysayers, who were telling me I needed to pay my bills and let God wait). I was too ashamed and too prideful to ask people for money back then. I was determined to make it on my own.

After I paid most of the bills besides my mortgage, I had thirty-five dollars left. Yes, thirty-five dollars. I had three choices: 1) I could call around and start begging for help. 2) I could break down in tears and curse God. 3) I could grow up and learn how to use my authority as a believer. I chose the latter. I got mad at the devil. I started praying the best I knew how to and decided to trust God. I remember saying, "You know what, Mr. Devil? I may not have a lot of money, but I do have Jesus, and you are not going to spoil our Christmas! We will celebrate the birth of our Lord!"

I took that thirty-five dollars to the dollar store. My children, my mother, and my pastor were on the top of my list. I didn't even stop to think how pitiful those presents would probably look to those who would receive them. I was determined to have Christmas no matter what. I bought thirty-three items, including a bag of bows and two boxes of Christmas cards. In the basket was a Christmas cup. I remember thinking, "He who gives a cup of water to a prophet in the name of the prophet will receive a prophet's reward." That is based on Matthew 10:41–42, which I was studying at the time.

Well, my pastor was a prophet, so I gave him the cup. I should have also bought him a bottle of water, but I didn't think of it at the time. I gave out the gifts and the cards, and the breakthrough was almost instant. The day before Christmas the children's spiritual godfather called and asked me what I was buying the children for Christmas. Not wanting to speak outside of my newfound faith, I answered, "God will provide."

Well, wouldn't you know, he read between the lines and came over just in time to take me shopping for new clothes for the children. With his gifts and my dollar-store toys and books, they had presents for Christmas. I decided right then, when I was putting the bow on that cup, that for the rest of that year I would dig in my heels, take out my notepad, and study everything my pastor was teaching because I knew he had something I needed.

A few years after that I graduated from our school of ministry and have since been delivered from a "fiery bed of affliction" in an intensive care unit, been delivered from bankruptcy into a brand-new home with no down payment, received new cars, gone on mission trips around the world, launched King for America, been healed from the guilt and shame of abortion, founded Alveda King Ministries, and so much more.

Today I consider Pastor McNair one of the world's best Bible teachers, past or present. He taught his flock the Word of God in such a way that we are becoming believers and doers of the Word. He encouraged me to exercise my faith and launch my own ministry, King for America, which later became Alveda King Ministries. Our foundational scripture is "Have faith in God" (Mark 11:22). I also serve as pastoral associate with Priests for Life, and I remain in the music ministry at BBCC and am on the teaching staff. This is my faith in action.

Giving my pastor that cup was an act of faith, a little like the widow's mite. At least that's how it felt back then. Today God makes all grace abound to me so that always having, I am able to give gifts without reservation. I am so glad Jesus is Lord. My friends, "Have faith in God"! Our divine keys and our gifts are released to us when we release our faith, which works by love, believing we will receive all that God has for us.

SCRIPTURE REFLECTION

So then faith cometh by hearing, and hearing by the word of God.

—ROMANS 10:17, KJV

But without faith it is impossible to please him.

—HEBREWS 11:6, KJV

And all things, whatsoever ye shall ask in prayer, believing, ye shall receive.

—MATTHEW 21:22, KJV

And Jesus answering saith unto them, Have faith in God.

—MARK 11:22, KJV

For by grace are ye saved through faith; and that not of yourselves: it is the gift of God.

—EPHESIANS 2:8–9, KJV

For with God nothing shall be impossible.

—LUKE 1:37, KJV

Now faith is the substance of things hoped for, the evidence of things not seen.

—HEBREWS 11:1, KJV

If you do not believe then you will not endure.

—ISAIAH 7:9, LEB

Faith [works] expressing itself through love.

—GALATIANS 5:6, NIV

PERSONAL REFLECTION

How strong is your faith?

PRAYER

Dear heavenly Father, I believe. Please help my unbelief. Help me truly believe and allow You to increase my faith. Allow me to successfully walk and live by faith, which works through Your love. In Jesus's name, by the power of Your Holy Spirit, I pray. Amen.

Chapter 7

DIVINE OBEDIENCE

What is more pleasing to the LORD: your burnt offerings and sacrifices or your obedience to his voice? Listen! Obedience is better than sacrifice, and submission is better than offering the fat of rams.

—1 SAMUEL 15:22

TRUE WORSHIP OF God requires obedience to God. Added to this truth should be the revelation that obedience to God is strengthened by submission to God. The first commandment with a promise attached to it centers around obedience:

> Honor your father and your mother, that your days may be long in the land that the LORD your God is giving you.
> —EXODUS 20:12, ESV

We see it again in the New Testament, and the blessing is called out.

> Children, obey your parents because you belong to the Lord, for this is the right thing to do. "Honor your father and mother." This is the first commandment with a promise: If you honor your father and mother, "things will go well for you, and you will have a long life on the earth." Fathers, do not provoke your children to anger by the way you treat them. Rather, bring them up with the discipline and instruction that comes from the Lord.
> —EPHESIANS 6:1–4

We see in the New Testament passage that further instructions are given to the fathers to train their children in the ways of God. In reading these scriptures, we begin to understand that children must be taught to love, honor, and obey divine authority. Divine love, the master key, comes into play in this process.

Christian author Oswald Chambers describes how truth is accessed by obedience:

> All of God's revealed truths are sealed until they are opened to us through obedience....God will never reveal more truth about Himself to you, until you have obeyed what you know already.[1]

Have you ever used a key that would fit into a lock but would not turn the tumbler? Such is the case with obedience and submission. They are two different keys: obedience opens the first lock, and submission opens the dead bolt.

Recently three of my prayer partners had a text conversation in which they discussed the covenant of obedience. They noted that blessings and curses are attached to our obedience. In passages such as Jeremiah 11 through 15 when God curses the disobedient, He is simply honoring the covenant He made with His people.

Our covenant with God does not excuse disobedience or shield us from its consequences. That is why we must repent when we disobey. As my prayer partners wrote in their series of texts, "A covenant nation that forsakes God, kills millions of children, promotes sexual immorality on a vast scale, and is greedy cannot expect a covenant-keeping God to bless it. But rather it should expect a covenant-keeping God to discipline it severely—quite severely, if it keeps ignoring warnings from God to stop the disobedience."[2]

They are so right. Divine obedience is a major key to seeing God's plans for our lives fulfilled.

THE DIFFERENCE BETWEEN SUBMISSION AND OBEDIENCE

Submit means "to give over or yield to the power or authority of another; to present for the approval, consideration, or decision of another or others: to submit a plan; to submit an application."[3] *Obey*, on the other hand, means "to comply with or follow the commands, restrictions, wishes, or instructions of; to comply with or follow (a command, restriction, wish, instruction, etc.)."[4]

Discussing these words in the context of marriage, blogger Sunny Shell noted that "by definition, submission is a far greater thing than obedience. Submission requires love, respect and a willingness to yield to another. Obedience on the other hand doesn't require any personal relationship between the one giving the 'command' and the one obeying the command."[5]

Touching on "sore spots" that often lead to rocky roads and bumpy, prickly trails in the marriage journey, Shell's analysis of the two words sometimes steps on my toes. One such irritant is the "obey" clause in the woman's marriage vows.

I can remember a major mistake that affected my life and marriages throughout the years. I vehemently objected to the "love and obey" clause of the marriage vows I was required to repeat at the altar. My groom was charged to "love and cherish." I was charged to "love and obey." My grandfather officiated at my wedding, and I respected him enough not to publicly cross him during the ceremony. But I crossed my fingers as I spoke the words, telling myself that such requirements were antiquated. What I didn't consider is that the Word of God never fades. Like the One who inspired the men of God to write it, the words of God are the same today, yesterday, and forever.

Ephesians 5:21–33 gives us divine guidance on the issue of submission in marriage:

> And further, submit to one another out of reverence for Christ.
>
> For wives, this means submit to your husbands as to the Lord. For a husband is the head of his wife as Christ is the head of the church. He is the Savior of his body, the church. As the church submits to Christ, so you wives should submit to your husbands in everything.
>
> For husbands, this means love your wives, just as Christ loved the church. He gave up his life for her to make her holy and clean, washed by the cleansing of God's word. He did this to present her to himself as a glorious church without a spot or wrinkle or any other blemish. Instead, she will be holy and without fault. In the same way, husbands ought to

love their wives as they love their own bodies. For a man who loves his wife actually shows love for himself. No one hates his own body but feeds and cares for it, just as Christ cares for the church. And we are members of his body.

As the Scriptures say, "A man leaves his father and mother and is joined to his wife, and the two are united into one." This is a great mystery, but it is an illustration of the way Christ and the church are one. So again I say, each man must love his wife as he loves himself, and the wife must respect her husband.

Having never read the Bible passage previously quoted, I felt the instructions to obey my husband were one-sided. I didn't know he would be required to submit to me as well, or that in submitting one to another, we could truly become one and overcome the world.

No, I didn't know or understand that obeying and submitting were to be a beautiful mutual agreement, that the man's responsibility would be even greater than my own, and that he would have to love me and treat me as if I were his own body. So I missed a perfect opportunity to enter marital bliss.

As a teenage bride on the verge of womanhood, with the rumblings of the women's rights movement at my heels, I was ready, with many of America's female baby boomers, to reject God's plan for harmony between the sexes. In other words, I felt women didn't need to bow down to men. We needed to be free. How in the world did I know back then that such freedom would include freedom to abort my babies, freedom to engage in uncommitted sexual relationships, and freedom to abandon God's plan for everything and go my own way?

Perhaps the most important point here is that obedience is just the beginning of a good marriage to God or to a mate. Somehow the two are closely related—obedience in marriage to a spouse and marriage to God—and can be critical keys to lasting joy.

Mrs. Anna McNair, the lifelong marriage partner to my beloved mentor, Pastor McNair, has been teaching the secrets of the Proverbs 31 woman to the women of our congregation for years. One of Mrs. Anna's mainstay reference books is *Fascinating Womanhood* by Helen Andelin. Mrs. Anna wins the women over using personal examples from her own marriage, or she at least entices them to try the lessons on for size.

Oh, how the young women laughed at first when they read the sections from Andelin's book on the joys of obedience and submission, first to God's Word and then to a husband. Yet once they began to try the credos and discover how powerful, effective, and genuine the principles in the book are for building a successful marriage, they were won over.

STRUGGLING WITH OBEDIENCE

This same process holds true in learning to obey, submit to, surrender to, and finally truly love God. And let's not fool ourselves. Marriage isn't the only area that causes people to struggle with obedience. There are many other strongholds couched in disobedience that can hinder Christians from experiencing greater spiritual success and liberty in their lives.

Obedience in forgiveness

We covered forgiveness in an earlier chapter. As we studied that key, we discovered that holding a grudge can cause serious damage to our lives, including the hindrance of our prayers. Forgiveness is an act of obedience. We are commanded to forgive. It is not a suggestion.

Obedience with money

Another area of disobedience that can keep us from unlocking our spiritual potential involves how we handle our money. Disobedience in tithing is a major issue among Christians. For some reason people resent teachings on responsible Christian stewardship, financial giving, and tithing. Through the ages people have left their churches and some have even walked away from the Christian faith over God's tithe. Many become so indignant regarding the tithe that they fall away from the faith. They are missing the point by believing that God is after their money.

KING FAMILY TRUTH

"Make thankfulness your sacrifice to God, and keep the vows you made to the Most High. Then call on me when you are in trouble, and I will rescue you, and you will give me glory."

—Psalm 50:14–15

To the contrary, God doesn't need our money:

> O my people, listen as I speak....But I do not need the bulls from your barns or the goats from your pens. For all the animals of the forest are mine, and I own the cattle on a thousand hills. I know every bird on the mountains, and all the animals of the field are mine. If I were hungry, I would not tell you, for all the world is mine and everything in it....Make thankfulness your sacrifice to God, and keep the vows you made to the Most High. Then call on me when you are in trouble, and I will rescue you, and you will give me glory.
>
> —PSALM 50:7, 9–12, 14–15

God desires our love, our faith, and our obedience. We can easily avoid this pitfall of disobeying the heavenly calling to give and tithe by applying the key of divine obedience to issues involving our finances.

The apostle Paul told the church at Philippi:

It's not that I'm looking for a gift. The opposite is true. I'm
looking for your resources to increase.
—PHILIPPIANS 4:17, GW

I once heard evangelist Laura Pickett explain that giving is a
heart issue because it demonstrates where our trust is. Brothers
and sisters, as we consider the key of divine obedience, we must
seek to obey God in all things according to His holy Word. This
includes matters of the heart and the wallet.

SCRIPTURE REFLECTION

Taste and see that the LORD is good. Oh, the joys of those
who take refuge in him!
—PSALM 34:8
(SEE ALSO PROVERBS 3, MALACHI 4, GALATIANS 6)

PERSONAL REFLECTION

Was there a time in your life when obedience was a challenge
for you? What was the issue? How did you resolve it? Are you
facing another challenge in the area of divine obedience? What
will you do?

PRAYER

*Lord, teach me to understand Your purpose for obedi-
ence and to accept Your plan for my life, which is for
my good. I pray in Jesus's name. Amen.*

Chapter 8

DIVINE SUBMISSION

Therefore submit to God. Resist the devil and he will flee from you.

—James 4:7, NKJV

D IVINE SUBMISSION IS submission to the Lord and to others according to God's will. In the chapter titled "Divine Obedience" we saw that submission was the next step. We talked about acts of obedience and submission within human relationships as well as to God. In this chapter we are looking more closely at submission between us and God. We learn and practice submission to God by learning to submit to one another. This process is rather symbiotic.

Submission to God should quickly follow acts of obedience to God. Following this path will make your journey less painful and more joyful. The constant struggle with your mind, emotions, and flesh as you reason why you don't need to submit to God will wear you out, likely sooner than later.

Although many consider submission to be an act of defeat or weakness, genuine submission is a decisive act of the will. The submission we are discussing in this chapter is not a universal concept, as in submission to anything for any reason. We are speaking of a very special category of submission—submission to God.

Jesus Christ—by the perfect example He set in His birth, life, death, and resurrection—has defined for us perfect submission through His relationship with God the Father and the Holy Spirit. Their relationship is the basis for any approach to spiritual submission.

Even the example of submission between husband and wife is not a universal model of submission. This level of submission is a biblical model, so only those who choose to live out these Bible principles would see the benefits of this type of submission in their lives. Without the power of God the Father, Jesus the Son, and the Holy Spirit as the anchor, submission would just be a joke or a dream for the human experience.

Within the biblical construct, submission isn't just for women. Men have a responsibility to submit as well. As author Mary Kassian noted in her blog "7 Misconceptions About Submission," all believers, male and female, have a responsibility to submit to the Lord and to the authorities He places in our lives. In chapter 4, "Divine Authority," we were reminded that for believers, submission and authority are connected.

Kassian, a professor of women's studies at Southern Baptist Theological Seminary, wrote that submission is something we choose to give to someone else; it's not a right to be demanded. For example, a husband does not have the right to demand that his wife submit to him. We each must choose to submit; it is a scriptural responsibility that comes with benefits. Those benefits are clearly defined by God, with the greatest reward being to receive love, even as Christ loved the church.[1]

In a marriage between believers—one man and one woman— deciding when and how to submit is a mutual call. Here the focus is not on personal rights but on personal responsibility. That being said, as the head of the union the husband has the greater responsibility, which is to love his wife sacrificially, just as Christ loves the church.[2] This means to love her, not force his wife to submit. By trusting God to direct her husband in what is best for the union, the wife is able to submit without rancor or competition. That sounds too simple, doesn't it?

Submitted isn't a synonym for *doormat.* A believer's first responsibility, male or female, is to submit to God's standard of righteousness. Kassian makes an important point in saying the wife's call to submit to her husband is never a call to submit to sin or abuse. God does not desire "weak-willed" women who lack the wisdom, strength, and courage needed to participate in godly unions. God's daughters should never be expected to submit to sin.[3]

Genesis 1 tells us that in the beginning God created man—and "male and female created he them" (v. 27, KJV). So the (hu)man of the Bible appears on the planet in two forms, male and female.

The church world as we know it has taken the fallen doctrine of men ruling over women (a result of the curse of the law from which Jesus has redeemed all believers) and attempted to make it a divine order. In Genesis, God cursed Adam and Eve by causing Adam to rule over Eve and Eve to experience pain in childbirth. God then turned Eve's desire away from Him and toward Adam.

When Eve lost the blessing of having her desires met by God and not her husband, a longing and an emptiness were created within her because Adam was never designed to meet Eve's needs. Only the Messiah, Jesus, can satisfy a longing soul, whether male or female. So fallen, unredeemed Adam assumed the position of having to rule over fallen, unredeemed Eve. Prior to the Fall, Adam ruled over birds and animals. After the Fall, Adam was cursed to rule Eve. Unredeemed men rule other people. Redeemed men lead others.

God doesn't operate by gender but rather through His anointing, which He imparts upon people. The prophet Joel plainly reminded us that in the latter days sons and daughters of man would prophesy. Echoing Joel 2:28, God decrees in Acts 2:17: "'In the last days...I will pour out my Spirit upon all people. Your sons and daughters will prophesy. Your young men will see visions, and your old men will dream dreams.'"

We are all spirit beings. Some of us are housed in female bodies, and some are in male bodies, yet there is no gender in the spirit. After all, the first evangelist after the resurrection of Jesus the Messiah was a woman named Mary Magdalene (Matt. 28:1–7; Mark 16).

Yet in a "redeemed" setting the husband is truly the priest of the home. It is written that we are all royal priests and priestesses, a chosen generation (1 Pet. 2:9). But Scripture also makes it clear that the husband is the head of the home (Eph. 5:22–24). God has specific realms of authority here on earth, and none of them overlap or contradict any others.

The husband is the pastor in the family, being the authority over his home. But he wouldn't have authority over the church unless he is the pastor of the local church. Women who are not going to church or who attend church sporadically should never use the excuse "My husband won't let me go to church." Women should obey and agree with their husbands according to what is legal in the natural and the spirit. If a husband demands, for instance, that his wife sells drugs for him, she is not honor bound to do that.

Consider this true example: A woman was driving a car, and her husband was on the passenger side. He demanded that she speed because they were in a hurry. Though the woman was not in agreement with speeding, she yielded to her husband's demand and soon got pulled over. When the police officer stopped her, he didn't ask for her husband's driver's license. He asked for hers, and she was the one who got the ticket. As it happens, her husband refused to help pay the fine.

The emphasis here is on the fact that the woman—not her husband—had to answer for her actions. Wives must follow their husbands as they follow Christ, but they do not have to follow them if their directives are illegal or inaccurate or go against the common law of the land and the will and Word of God.

Men and women must seek deep relationships with God to comprehend more of God's character and nature so they will know what is proper and improper. One way to get to know God better and discover more of His character is by studying the meaning of His many names listed in the Bible. God is known as

God the Father, God the Son, and God the Holy Spirit, so there are many names of God that can be studied. (See the list near the end of the chapter.) Take your time, and enjoy the courtship!

> Oh, that we might [follow on to] know the LORD! Let us press on to know him. He will respond to us as surely as the arrival of dawn or the coming of rains in early spring.
>
> —HOSEA 6:3

In really getting to know God and pursuing Him, we must not be complacent. We must be excited about developing a true relationship with Him. In Isaiah 32 women are warned not to be complacent. In the Book of Titus women are charged to be godly. I only mention the women's perspective here because I'm a woman. Men are equally charged to be diligent in pursuit of truth.

In the second chapter of Colossians we as men and women of God are reminded of our rightful positions. Verses 11–14 say that when we came to Christ, He set us free from our evil desires (our unfulfilled longings). We were dead in sins, and our sinful (cursed) desires were not yet cut away. Then He gave us a share in the very life of Christ, for He forgave all our sins and blotted out the charges proved against us (a result of the curse of Adam and Eve and the breaking of God's commandments).

Jesus took the list of sins (and curses) and destroyed it by nailing it to the cross. Jesus reached His maturity and ministry during His life on earth, whereas Adam and Eve never reached maturity because they allowed rebellion to hinder them. Their basic sin stemmed from wanting to be independent of God, and it led to disobedience.

God wants to pour Himself into us. He gave us breath. Then He prepared a way for us to be redeemed and given eternal life. In a unique covenant among the Trinity, God made arrangements for us to live with Him forever. If we are to be included in that covenant, we must first surrender to God.

The tree of the knowledge of good and evil includes humanism, atheism, skepticism, Communism, new age, women's lib, sexual depravity, and every other Christless thought we can imagine. The woman was named Eve—mother of all the living—after the Fall, but she was redeemed so she could bring forth a seed that would eventually destroy the devil.

Just as he did in the garden, Satan's attack against mankind is still couched in deception. Satan first stole Eve, the bride of His first son. Satan now pursues the second bride, Christ's bride, which is the church. The only difference is that Adam was not Jesus, who has the power to protect His bride.

When Adam's bride sinned, Adam followed suit. That's not the case with us. When the bride of Christ sins, He leads us to repentance and back to God. Even after we repent, we must stay alert and continue to resist Satan. As long as we are on this earth, we will face trials. Christ said: "I have told you these things, so that in me you may have peace. In this world you will have trouble. But take heart! I have overcome the world" (John 16:33, NIV).

KING FAMILY TRUTH

As we submit to God's plan for us, all our needs are met and our desires can be fulfilled.

Jesus overcame and defeated Satan for us. We still must resist him, but we don't have to fight with carnal weapons. We have the armor of God! (See Ephesians 6.) As we submit to God's plan for us, all our needs are met and our desires can be fulfilled.

OUR SUBMISSION TO GOD CAN LEAD OTHERS TO HIM

I want to share a testimony of how a husband's turning of the key of divine submission to God led his wife to Christ. Together they found God's plan for their marriage and understanding of the mystery of submission.

My husband had a fiery temper and I was stubborn. The submission taught in the Bible was a joke, an actual offense to me. I didn't want a man telling me what to do. What a pair we were.

Then my dear husband met Jesus. All alone, on the front porch of our home, he cried out: "God, if You are real, then show Yourself." My husband went inside, sat on the edge of our bed, and there, in his solitude, God came to him, and revealed Jesus. Not just the storybook Jesus, but the life-changing Jesus.

After that life-changing experience, my husband shoved aside all of his other books on how to be rich and successful, on black power, astrology, and all other psychology and religion topics. He started reading the Bible, day in and day out. He played Kenneth Copeland tapes so much that I couldn't stand it. It didn't matter. He kept on reading and listening.

He was truly being transformed before my very eyes! I didn't believe it at first. I thought it was just another one of his schemes. But he kept on changing, or the Lord kept transforming his old sin nature.

Finally one day I began to want to change too. I wanted what he was getting. So I too gave my life to Jesus. Once my husband and I both decided to serve the Lord together, our whole life together turned around.

I wanted to be like the woman in Proverbs 31. We started going to Bible study and a holiness church. I guess at first my zeal carried me to the limits. For a while, I didn't wear lipstick, didn't style my hair. I was hungry for the truth. As time went on, I began to grow up in the Word, to know that I am to be a beautiful example of God's love and grace.

Then I began to share this good news with other women, to see their lives changed and their marriages restored. This was all very wonderful until God told my husband to leave his career and go full time into the ministry. Over the years, we had graduated from food stamps and an apartment to high-salaried positions, a lovely home, and nice cars.

I wasn't aware how important these things were to me until the call came. I thought back to the day when my husband had demanded (after six months of using food stamps) that we stop using welfare. "I am a man!" he insisted. "We will not live this way!" He always worked, but sometimes it had been hard to make it, so I had gotten the food stamps without consulting him. He hated eating cabbage and gristle hamburgers, but he hated food stamps even more. I am glad he did. Within a short period he turned our circumstances around.

This was early in our marriage. I guess as I reflected on how God had delivered us from food stamps, I began to realize that I could trust Him to carry us into wherever He was leading us now.

The "wherever" continues to expand. God met our needs from the very moment we stepped out into the unknown. There were stormy moments. We have had to learn faith and live by faith. But the fruit of the promise is real in our life. We now have a beautiful marriage, three beautiful children who all live for the Lord, and an extended family as pastors of a church with a growing congregation.

I do not regret one moment of my life. The love I share with my husband is more than I could ever have imagined. The Bible says that if I am a godly woman, I will do my husband good and not evil all the days of our lives. I obey and submit to my husband as he submits to God. I do not feel ruled and dominated. I know I am loved. My precious husband often says I am his best friend. He truly is my best friend. Together Jesus is the center of our joy. We go on together in Christ, from glory to glory.[4]

Glory to God! There is so much to be learned about divine submission. As believers we should grow in submission to God's Word, to our spouses, and to one another. As we do, others will see Christ in us, and lives can be changed for the good. Selah.

THE NAMES OF GOD

Have you praised God today? Take a few moments with God by calling God's names and attributes as you worship the King in spirit and in truth. There is always more to discover about God, so feel free to add to the list.

Lord God, You are:

Wonderful	My Fortress
Counselor	The Prince of Peace
The Rock of Ages	The King of glory
The Lion of Judah	Mighty
The King of kings	My Shield
Merciful	Gracious
Faithful	Giving
The Balm of Gilead	El Elyon, God Most High
Jehovah Rapha, the Lord our Healer	Jehovah Rohi, the Lord our Shepherd
Jehovah Jireh, the Lord our Provider	Jehovah Tsidkenu, the Lord our Righteousness
Jehovah Shammah, the Lord who is present	Jehovah Shalom, the Lord our Peace
My Creator	The master Potter
My Teacher	My Comforter
My Redeemer	The Miracle Worker

Invincible	The Hope of glory
The Lamb of God	The Light of the world
The Rose of Sharon	The Lord of lords
My Banner	The Bread of Life
All-consuming Fire	The Way
Omnipotent	The Truth
Omniscient	The Life
Omnipresent	My High Priest
My Deliverer	Wisdom
The great I Am	The Alpha and Omega
The living Word	The righteous Judge
My Protector	The Ancient of Days
The Commander of the heavenly hosts	The Author and Finisher of our faith
My Intercessor	El Olam, the everlasting God
El Gibor, God our Helper	My Savior

Truly there is no one like God! To Him be all the glory forever.

SCRIPTURE REFLECTION

During the days of Jesus' life on earth, he offered up prayers and petitions with fervent cries and tears to the one who could save him from death, and he was heard because of his reverent submission.

—HEBREWS 5:7, NIV

PERSONAL REFLECTION

Is there an area in your life where you have not submitted to the will of God? Will you pray for guidance?

PRAYER

Heavenly Father, I have not always understood the importance of submission. Please help me submit to You and to others according to Your will and Your Word. I pray in Jesus's name. Amen.

To hear Alveda King's song
"The Lord Is Here,"
scan the QR code
or visit
https://tinyurl.com/TheLordIsHere.

Chapter 9

DIVINE SURRENDER

Then Peter began to speak up. "We've given up everything to follow you," he said.

—MARK 10:28

OFTEN WHEN WE think of surrender, we think of someone who has lost a battle and is waving a white flag. Or we visualize a person in the face of eminent domination, lifting up his or her arms and hands and saying, "Don't shoot!" Such acts of surrender often happen among humans in acts of war, terror, or danger, though there are other ways surrender to human authority manifests.

To surrender means "to yield (something) to the possession or power of another; deliver up possession of on demand or under duress: to surrender the fort to the enemy; to surrender the stolen goods to the police."[1] It can also mean "to give (oneself) up, as to the police."[2]

Surrendering to God is different from surrendering to human authority. When we surrender to God, we give up, abandon, or relinquish ourselves—our carnality, our pride, and the like. And we are yielding or resigning our own power or privilege in favor of another, higher authority.[3]

I'll be the first to tell you that surrendering to God isn't easy. Some come joyfully, while others come kicking and screaming. No matter how we come to Him, we have to do the surrendering. God will not force anyone to surrender. There's a song that says, "Softly and tenderly Jesus is calling…calling, O sinner, come home!"[4] That is true. In His loving-kindness He draws us to the place of surrender. But He will sometimes use circumstances that don't feel so good. For instance, God can allow a cushy job to become a nightmare or a familiar place to seem like a desert. Yet this is not coercion. It's more like a mother bird pushing her baby bird out of the nest. God wants us to get so uncomfortable that our only recourse is to run to Him—and find freedom.

THE SONG OF SURRENDER

My path to surrender came through the notes of beautiful songs of praise and worship. There's something about music that opens the pathways of the heart. That's why I believe some of my most memorable moments of surrendering more and more of myself to God happened during times of worship. The Christian hymn "I Surrender All" has been a familiar and comforting staple in my musical arsenal. I remember singing it as a girl at the Baptist church we attended as a family. You may have heard it at a church you attended as well. This hymn is one that will touch your heartstrings.

There are other songs that also lead me into deep worship: "There Is No One Else Like You (You Deserve the Glory)," "All Glory," "I Love You, Lord," "Draw Me Close to You," and so many more. In the early 1990s ministers Bruce and Cindy Black came to my church and sang "You Deserve the Glory." The song has been one of my favorites ever since. It immediately brings me to a place of surrender to God's will for my life.

I took a step closer to God on March 28, 2016, while I was on the phone talking with a close friend. Having taken a liking to bursting into song anywhere, anytime, as was often done in the Broadway musical films I enjoyed watching on television during my early years, I broke out in song right in the middle of our conversation. I began to sing "You Deserve the Glory."

Suddenly, while I was singing, it hit me: I needed to go deeper, to surrender to God for real—completely—and not just sing the song. I stopped singing midline and told my friend that I had to hang up and connect with God. This was such a *kairos* moment— a time appointed by God! It was time to take a deeper plunge.

Oh, I had experienced moments of surrender in the past— surrendering to salvation and ministry calls, surrendering bad habits and many other things that distracted me from my devotion to God—but letting go in bits and pieces wasn't going to be enough anymore. That song caused me to hear the voice of the Spirit bidding me to let go and really allow God to have all of me.

Songs can help move the heart closer and closer to surrendering to God, but songs alone can't do it all. Our lives need to be an outward demonstration of what we pledge to God in those private moments of deep worship. After the song has been sung, are you still surrendered? Will you still give your all by what you say and do? Are you living proof that your heart has been completely given over to God?

THE JOURNEY TO SURRENDER

In *My Utmost for His Highest* Oswald Chambers speaks of Jesus's surrender at the end of His earthly ministry. Throughout His revealed ministry here on earth, Jesus was in total submission to God, His Father. He was obedient and submissive—our perfect example—and He surrendered His all to God, telling the Father, "I brought glory to you here on earth by completing the work you gave me to do" (John 17:4).

As Oswald Chambers writes, "Surrender is not the surrender of the external life, but of the will; when that is done, all is done." God will never crush us into surrender. Rather, "He waits until the man yields up his will to Him." Then "that battle never needs to be re-fought."[5]

As I mentioned earlier in this chapter, there can be a path, a journey to surrender. This process involves learning and agreeing to be obedient and submissive to God's will. Then there are specific areas of surrender. I first had to surrender to salvation, then the call to ministry, then to give up fleshly things that were important to me, such as an unnatural affection for food and a consuming appetite for soap operas and trashy television shows.

As human beings we all have these categories of carnality, even when we are in denial and believe our little issues aren't as bad as those of others. Many of us surrender our secret obsessions a little bit at a time. When we are brave, we can even go cold turkey and take deep plunges into God and just let go.

Surrender often comes after we grow weary of fighting God's will so we can have our way. Life can be a constant war—until we raise our hands and wave the flag of surrender.

Oswald Chambers defines *surrender* in three stages:

- "Surrender for deliverance"—The beginning stage of surrender that happens right after we give our lives to Christ and receive salvation. We learn that we can come to Him for rest and rescue from the enemy of our souls.

- "Surrender for devotion"—At this stage of surrender we pursue the person of Christ. Nothing else will do. This is also the stage where our lives begin to bear witness to that decision to surrender all.

- "Surrender for death" (John 21:18–19)—This is the stage of ultimate surrender unto death. Nothing in this life appeals to you except that which appeals to Christ. You are completely dead to self.[6]

This third level of surrender yields a desire for "unbroken communion with God," as Chambers puts it.[7] It's hard to imagine, when you think about it. But the Bible states that before the Fall, Adam experienced this level of glorious connection with God. Jesus came and made the ultimate sacrifice, the ultimate surrender, to restore to us the opportunity to experience this phenomenal intimate connection with God.

So how do we get there? We must let the Holy Spirit teach and guide us. The secret to truly surrendering to God is found in His Word, in spending time with the Holy Spirit. James 4:8 says if you draw near to God, He will draw near to you.

King Family Truth

If you draw near to God, He will draw near to you.

As we follow this path to surrender, we quickly discover that trust is a major factor. So many times I have been near total surrender, only to draw back at the last second. Yet in those moments I can sense God assuring me, saying, "Trust Me."

The Bible says, "Trust in the LORD with all your heart and lean not on your own understanding; in all your ways submit to him, and he will make your paths straight" (Prov. 3:5–6, NIV). Notice the passage says to trust God. We are not instructed to put our trust in people. Psalm 146:3 says, "Don't put your confidence in powerful people [or any mere human beings, for that matter]; there is no help for you there."

You can and should love people with the love of God, but do not trust or place your confidence in human beings. Flesh will always fail you. Your flesh is weak, as is the next person's. This is the case with all humans. Surrender your trust and your heart to God, and experience "unbroken communion" with Him.

Scripture Reflection

Therefore I urge you, brethren, by the mercies of God, to present your bodies a living and holy sacrifice, acceptable to God, which is your spiritual service of worship.

—Romans 12:1, NASB

PERSONAL REFLECTION

Chart out a plan for deeper surrender to God. Take small steps in that direction.

PRAYER

Father, surrender isn't easy. Help me reach out to You today. I pray in Jesus's name. Amen.

Chapter 10

DIVINE HUMILITY

God opposes the proud but gives grace to the humble.

—JAMES 4:6

THE BOOK OF Exodus introduces us to Moses, who in Numbers 12:3 is described as being "very meek, more than all people who were on the face of the earth" (ESV). The Bible never says Moses was perfect. He didn't get to see the Promised Land because he didn't exactly follow God's instructions when he struck the rock to release a flow of water for the grumbling Hebrews he had been born to liberate. Some people have assumed that Moses's striking of the rock rather than speaking to it is why he failed to make it to the Promised Land. But that wasn't the reason. It was his anger. He was meek and humble, except when he let his temper get the best of him.

In more modern times, during the twentieth century, my uncle ML was also known to be a humble man, seeking nonviolence in the face of war, racism, and controversy. During his lifetime he was often called the Black Moses. He was also called the apostle of love due to his teachings and modeling of agape love. In many ways Uncle ML was like Moses. He was a twentieth-century prophet and liberator. Also, just as Moses wasn't perfect, Uncle ML wasn't perfect. Both Moses and Uncle ML were imperfect men who served a perfect God.

Moses had his brother, Aaron, to help him. Uncle ML had Daddy. In their own manner Aaron and Daddy, in the struggles of their times, shared the mantles of faith, love, and humility that their brothers bore. Together they have gone down in history, known not for their deeds alone but also for their love of God.

Reminiscent of James and John in the Bible due to their fiery preaching styles, Uncle ML and Daddy were often called "the Sons of Thunder." People would even smile and say, "If they are the sons, their daddy must be the thunder." All three men were indeed fiery Baptist preachers. Their sermons always included the themes of agape love, faith, serving and caring for the least of these, and justice. Daddy and Uncle ML paid the ultimate price, laying down their earthly lives in the civil rights movement of the twentieth century. Yet through their obedience and submission to "the heavenly calling" they received the ultimate prize—eternal life.

> But among you it will be different. Whoever wants to be a leader among you must be your servant.
>
> —MATTHEW 20:26

During their lifetimes Moses and Martin were considered meek and humble servants of God. Yet they were never known as "weak" men. They serve as examples of how humility gives us great strength to fulfill the purpose God has for us.

IT'S NOT ABOUT ME

Humility is the quality or condition of being humble or to have a modest opinion or estimate of one's own importance or rank.[1] For Christians humility requires that we die to ourselves. This is not necessarily a physical death but a death of our fleshly and rebellious natures, as well as a submission of our wills to God's plan and purposes for our lives. Obedience and submission to God are examples of strength, not weakness.

Even our Lord Jesus Christ, the highest and most perfect example of humility, was never weak. Through Christ's examples of humility, obedience, and submission to God, His Father, He remains our High Priest and perfect example of the divine key of humility. Denying Himself, He went so far as to shed His blood for our sins, wrestle the keys of hell and death from our enemy Satan, and rise again.

On a personal note, my greatest challenge regarding humility is remembering that it's not about me. Putting my desires last is never easy. Perhaps the number one law of human nature is self-preservation. Having experienced many hard knocks and disappointments in my life, I learned over the years to shut out emotions and depend on myself to make things happen.

Too often people disappointed me by either dying on me or not living up to my expectations. Before being born again, I had a "What are you going to do for me?" type of mentality. I could see the motes in others' eyes without ever acknowledging that I had a beam blinding my own vision. I was always quick to find fault with others while denying my own. Does this sound familiar?

> And why worry about a speck in your friend's eye when you have a log in your own?
>
> —MATTHEW 7:3

I like what a good friend had to say about humility:

> Take self off the center stage, and put God there. A lot of people have different ideas about who we are in relation to God. I think it is most accurate to think of ourselves as incredibly blessed creatures whom God has given His own life to in love. This puts God on the center stage as the object of our attention, affection, and devotion. So talk to Him about everything. Listen to Him for all things. Follow His lead in every single thing. Live in, through, with, by, and because of Him.[2]

Along my life's journey I have often observed that the more gifted people are, the less inclined they are to serve others. Even though the Bible teaches us, "Freely you have received, freely give" (Matt. 10:8, NKJV), the opposite is often true. Rather than serving others, Christians often expect to be acknowledged and given preferential treatment because they are gifted.

Think about it: How many people with ministry gifts are willing to be part of the ministry of helps in their local churches? Oh, we are quick to point out how the Bible teaches that ministry gifts are special, and that's why God had His apostles seek out helpers to carry out the "ordinary work" of the church. Yet during His earthly ministry Jesus rolled up His sleeves and washed the feet of His disciples. There must be a balance that the servant-leader is willing to attain and maintain.

As human beings it's often hard for us to admit our own self-ishness. It took the reality of the ultimate, unselfish, and obe-dient blood sacrifice of Jesus Christ to cause me to look in shame on my own faults and to humble myself to accept Jesus as the gift, the key to my lasting joy and happiness. When I put Christ and others first, my joy is complete and my cup continues to overflow. This sounds impossible, doesn't it? Yet experience continues to prove this truth in my life.

King Family Truth

"Everybody can be great, because everybody can serve."[3]
—Martin Luther King Jr.

Life by a Thousand Blessings

There is a familiar saying that we can die a "death by a thousand cuts." In other words, we can experience many, many blows and pains in life and lose a little peace and joy with each attack, or something big can come along and knock us out of the game. By contrast, we can have "life by a thousand blessings" when we live the victorious albeit humble life in Christ. In other words, we can give up our personal agendas and learn to seek God's will for every single part of our beings—what to wear, what to eat, where to go, and what to do—forsaking our own way. Once we begin to do this, to die to self, we really begin to live in and for Him.

I die every day.

—1 Corinthians 15:31, ncv

Philippians 3:10–11 has long been my prayer: "I want to know Christ and experience the mighty power that raised him from the dead. I want to suffer with him, sharing in his death, so that one way or another I will experience the resurrection from the dead!" As a dear pastor friend of mine once said, "Dying is the price we must pay if we want to be raised from the dead to live and work and walk in the power of the [resurrection]. It all comes down to dying to self.... There must be a daily dying that must take place if we really want to live."[4]

SCRIPTURE REFLECTION

He leads the humble in what is right, and teaches the humble his way.

—PSALM 25:9, ESV

God will give ear and humble them, he who is enthroned from of old, Selah because they do not change and do not fear God.

—PSALM 55:19, ESV

Likewise, you who are younger, be subject to the elders. Clothe yourselves, all of you, with humility toward one another, for "God opposes the proud but gives grace to the humble."

—1 PETER 5:5, ESV

Have this mind among yourselves, which is yours in Christ Jesus, who, though he was in the form of God, did not count equality with God a thing to be grasped, but emptied himself, by taking the form of a servant, being born in the likeness of men. And being found in human form, he humbled himself by becoming obedient to the point of death, even death on a cross.

—PHILIPPIANS 2:5–8, ESV

Humble yourselves in the sight of the Lord, and he shall lift you up.

—JAMES 4:10, KJV

PERSONAL REFLECTION

Are you ready to die to your former self to live for God through Christ? Make a list of things in your life that you must "die" to.

PRAYER

Dear heavenly Father, by the power of Your Holy Spirit, teach me how to be Your humble servant—strong in You despite my weakness. In Jesus's name I pray. Amen.

Chapter 11

DIVINE PRAYER

Pray without ceasing.

—1 Thessalonians 5:17, kjv

THE HYMN "SWEET Hour of Prayer" has touched hundreds of thousands of people, as it expresses the incredible joy the songwriter found in prayer.

> Sweet hour of prayer! Sweet hour of prayer!
> That calls me from a world of care,
> And bids me at my Father's throne
> Make all my wants and wishes known.
> In seasons of distress and grief,
> My soul has often found relief,
> And oft escaped the tempter's snare,
> By thy return, sweet hour of prayer![1]

My first grown-up lesson on prayer came from Rev. Billy Graham during an interview when he was in Atlanta to lead a crusade. I was a journalism student at Georgia State University at the time and also working for *Lovely Atlanta* magazine as an independent reporter. I was impressed, not with him but with myself for landing an interview with such an important personality. At the time, I was too spiritually immature to realize the genuine honor of being allowed to interview a true man of God. I really didn't know what it meant to be a man of God, even though I had been raised by three prophets: Daddy, Granddaddy, and Uncle ML.

To make a long story short, I was allowed fifteen minutes with Rev. Graham. I remember asking him about his relationship with Uncle ML and how they had preached together in Madison Square Garden in the 1950s. Somehow he turned the conversation to the importance of prayer and said we must always "pray without ceasing." Of course, I didn't know he was speaking directly from Scripture, and I glibly responded with a chuckle, "Oh, Dr. Graham, no one can pray all of the time."

I'll never forget the clarity of his brilliant blue eyes and the agape love in his voice as he responded, "Alveda, I am praying for you now."

KING FAMILY TRUTH

"Pray without ceasing."

—1 Thessalonians 5:17, KJV

THE PILLAR OF PRAYER

Years later I joined BBCC, and Pastor McNair taught us that prayer is a major pillar in a successful Christian life. During the twenty-eight years I was mentored by Pastor McNair, prayer, along with faith, love, and daily Bible reading, became a steady diet for me. This remains my lifestyle today, and I sincerely recommend the same for you.

Pastor McNair used to say that unanswered prayer doesn't always mean no. It can mean wait. Or it can mean that we are praying amiss. (See James 4:3.) Another perspective is that there is no such thing as unanswered prayer. Jesus never spoke of God not answering our prayers. It may be that we try to minimize the heaviness of the answers as the Spirit of God calls us higher. As we discussed in the previous chapter, some things of God are not pleasant to our flesh. Prayer reveals to us the supernatural intent of the heart of God. If our hearts are too consumed with ourselves and worldly pleasures, could it be that unanswered prayer is really about our inability to discern the voice of God?

The Prayer Closet

He said to them, "It is written, 'My house shall be called a house of prayer,' but you make it a den of robbers."
—Matthew 21:13, esv

I have learned so much about prayer through the 6:00 a.m. prayer classes I've attended at my church and the prayer missions I've made to Africa and various parts of the United States, where I would join others in praying over territories. Learning about prayer in a community of prayer warriors has strengthened my prayer life and led me to develop a way to make prayer the center of my life and home.

Long before the popular film *War Room* released, I built prayer rooms in closets and corners in every house I have lived in. There is always an altar and several prayer boxes in these secret places in my home. It is important to have places set aside for prayer. Yet, as we'll discuss in the chapter on intimacy, the best secret place of prayer is in our hearts. We can't always wait to get to our prayer rooms to pray. We have to "pray without ceasing" anytime and anyplace.

If there are people in our lives we are troubled about—including family members, friends, church members, coworkers, politicians, you name it—we should pray for them. One of the greatest gifts we can give anyone is prayer. Even when others hurt us, the most effective solution is to forgive, pray, and find healing. As we release our prayers, even our enemies can be transformed by a change of heart, or what I like to call a "blood transfusion." The blood of Jesus covers a multitude of sins, and through our prayers God realigns the direst situations.

God's Ways Are Perfect

Sometimes it is hard to understand God's ways—why we have to wait for answers to prayer or why He doesn't respond to our petitions the way we were expecting. But we must remember that His ways are perfect, and He is always working things together for our good (Rom. 8:28). A friend recently reminded me of this truth when he shared with me a story that is often told.

> A king had a male servant who, no matter the circumstance, always said to him, "My king, do not be discouraged because everything God does is perfect. He makes no mistakes." One day the two men went hunting, and a wild animal attacked the king. The servant managed to kill the animal but couldn't prevent his majesty from losing a finger. Furious over his injury, the king said, "If God was good, I would not have been attacked and lost one finger." To this the servant replied, "Despite all these things, I can only tell you that God is good and everything He does is perfect. He is never wrong." Outraged by this response, the king ordered that the servant be arrested. As he was being taken to prison, the servant told the king again, "God is good and perfect."
>
> On another day, the king left alone for another hunt and was captured by savages who used human beings for sacrifice. When they had the king on the altar, the savages discovered that he was lacking one finger. Because the king was deemed not "complete" and therefore unfit to be offered to their gods, the savages released him. Upon his return to the palace, the king ordered the release of his servant and said, "My friend, God was really good to me. I was almost killed, but for lack of a single finger I was let go. But I have a question, If God is so good, why did He allow me to put you in prison?"
>
> His servant replied, "My king, if I had not been put in prison, I would have gone with you, and I would have been sacrificed because I have no missing finger. Everything God does is perfect. He is never wrong."

We can always trust God's ways, even when we don't understand them. As my friend told me, we often complain about the negative things that happen in life, forgetting that everything happens for a purpose. God knows exactly what you need and when you need it. He is good and perfect.

My friend went on to say:

> A good attitude will determine your altitude. When you look at your life, career, job, or family life, what do you say? Do you praise God? Do you blame Satan? A good attitude toward God makes Him move on your behalf. Just sit down and say, "Today I am thankful I had a peaceful sleep. I am thankful I am alive with possibilities. I am thankful I have a roof over me. I am thankful I have a job. I am thankful I have family and friends. Above all, I am thankful that I have God in my life."
>
> Don't be envious or shocked when others are prospering because you don't know what tests, trials, and tribulation they have endured to get there. So thank God for what you have. Little is much when God is in it. If God is for you, who can be against you?[2]

God works in us and in our situations when we seek Him in prayer. This is how we deepen our intimacy with Him and become more like Him.[3]

SCRIPTURE REFLECTION

The LORD is far from the wicked, but he hears the prayers of the righteous.

—PROVERBS 15:29

PERSONAL REFLECTION

For whom can you pray? How can you commit to blessing them? How can you regularly remember to do so? What emotions can you overcome through prayer? What issues can be resolved through God's work?

PRAYER

Our Father which art in heaven, hallowed be thy name. Thy kingdom come, Thy will be done in earth, as it is in heaven. Give us this day our daily bread. And forgive us our debts, as we forgive our debtors. And lead us not into temptation, but deliver us from evil: For thine is the kingdom, and the power, and the glory, for ever. Amen.

—Matthew 6:9–13, kjv

To hear Alveda King's song "Heaven Comes to Me," which relates to prayer, scan the QR code or visit https://tinyurl.com/HeavenComestoMe.

Chapter 12

DIVINE PRAISE AND WORSHIP

Every song is not a worship song. Every singer [or dancer, or musician] is not a worshiper. Although God never imparts the spiritual giftings and anointing of the singing voice and the skillful use of musical instruments or the dance for use as an entertainment tool, what should be spiritual singing sadly all too often has been used for entertainment. The sounds emanating from our instruments of praise and worship should come across the airwaves into the atmosphere being released and received as if God is speaking if we are indeed working on His behalf.[1]

—PROPHETESS S. ELAINE CLAY

As a child growing up, I didn't give much thought to the concept of worship. Almost from the cradle I spontaneously sang and talked to God without much prompting. Thankfully as a PK (preacher's kid) I knew about God and learned many Bible verses in Sunday school. So I grew up having the Word of God near me, sometimes even in my mouth and in my heart. Growing up as a PK has its advantages.

I have learned that together praise and worship are a powerful key that unlocks our spiritual gifts. God is ever calling His people to worship Him in spirit and in truth. When we realize this, we will understand the vital need to practice genuine divine praise and worship in our daily lives.

Praise is the highest form of spiritual warfare. The Bible says God inhabits our praises (Ps. 22:3). And in John 1:51 Jesus declared, "I tell you the truth, you will all see heaven open and the angels of God going up and down on the Son of Man, the one who is the stairway between heaven and earth." This tells me that when we praise God, the heavens open, angels ascend and descend, and God dwells within our praises.

There is a song called "Break Every Chain," and the lyrics call us to listen for the sound of chains falling. Often when I am ministering that song, both as a soloist and as a member of the congregation, I literally hear chains falling and demons fleeing in frustration as yokes of sickness, poverty, emotional distress, and other situations break in the spirit. We enter these realms through the name of Jesus, the power of His blood, and the authority we have as worshipping and praising believers operating in faith and agape love.

Consider this: in the Bible God sent the dancers, musicians, and singers out ahead of the weapon-bearing armies to defeat Israel's enemies. Can you imagine today's military being led by a host of praising worshippers? What demon is going to mess with that army?

Many of us have a general concept of what praise and worship are. What we don't always realize is that aside from obedience— avoiding sin and doing what God asks of us—there are specific ways to demonstrate our admiration and affection for God and our submission to Him in worship.

In Scripture as we read of David's many great exploits, we also get a glimpse into ancient worship practices that are still applicable today. David was the author of numerous psalms, and for many his way of worshipping God has become the "ideal" way to worship. Yet because there are so many other examples of genuine worship in the Bible, we can conclude that while David is one of the greatest worshippers of all time, he is not the final word on the subject.

Still, we have much to learn from David, who was a master of praise and a true worshipper. In 1 Chronicles 16 he presents a model for worship that can help us practice this divine key each day. After David and his comrades journeyed to Obed-edom to bring back the ark of the covenant—the symbol of Yahweh's provision and advocacy for His people—David placed the ark in the special tent they had prepared for it, and he presented burnt offerings and peace offerings to God. Then "he appointed some of the Levites as ministers before the ark of the LORD, to invoke, to thank, and to praise the LORD, the God of Israel" (1 Chron. 16:4, ESV).

We see in this verse that the Levites, the tribe designated as religious teachers, first invoked Yahweh. Then they did what should be natural in all our encounters with God: they thanked and then praised Him.

These ascending acts show us how we should worship:

1. Acknowledge God by calling on Him.

2. Thank Him for His provision.

3. Praise Him for who He is.

Only after thanking and praising God did David make his petition, saying: "Save us, O God of our salvation! Gather and rescue us from among the nations, so we can thank your holy name and rejoice and praise you. Praise the LORD, the God of Israel, who lives from everlasting to everlasting!" (1 Chron. 16:35–36).

Many times we do the opposite. We petition God without ever acknowledging Him or thanking Him for what He has already done. We must be ever mindful that we don't praise God because He needs to hear how great He is. We praise and worship Him because *we* need to be reminded of His power and goodness. God desires what is best for us, and He desires our praise and worship because they are for our good.

KING FAMILY TRUTH

We don't praise God because He needs to hear how great He is. We praise and worship Him because we need to be reminded of His power and goodness.

By humbling ourselves before Him in praise and worship, we are demonstrating our rightful place in His kingdom as His servants who are appointed to do great works for Him (Eph. 1:11; 2:10). We are showing that we are mindful of His love toward us, which is what God desires to see in us.

Worship is really about longing for God and acknowledging that we belong to Him. Our attitude toward God should be as Psalm 84:2 proclaims: "My soul longs and even fails for the courtyards of Yahweh. My heart and flesh sing for joy to the living God" (LEB).

TRUE WORSHIP

I believe I was closer to true worship as a child than I have sometimes been as an adult. For years after I grew up, I searched for truth in my own way. I kept asking people about worship because I wanted to understand what it truly meant. I read religious books, attended spiritual conferences, and studied the religions of the world because I was hungry to experience true worship. Now I realize that I was making my quest more complicated than it had to be. It wasn't until I was born again that truth began to come into my heart and quiet my longings. I began to truly feed on the Word of God and learn to genuinely worship my Lord.

What is true worship? True worship is the transparent expression of our submission and obedience to God as a child to a parent. In our case the "in spirit and in truth" worship relationship Jesus seeks is between God and us—His children, His workmanship. So the next question should perhaps be, How can we worship someone we do not know? Jesus once told a woman in the Bible, "You worship what you do not know.... But the hour is coming, and is now here, when the true worshipers will worship the Father in spirit and truth" (John 4:22–23, ESV).

We see throughout the Scriptures that many men and women discovered the hard way that there is a God in heaven. I think of Pharaoh, who refused to release God's people from bondage in Egypt, and the prophets of Baal, who died when God rained down fire from heaven. If we are wise, we will learn the consequences of rejecting God through the experiences of those who would not submit to the sovereignty of the one true God.

We can also learn from those who chose to love, serve, and obey God. Their testimonies can become our examples for living. As our Bible heroes came to know and follow God in the fullness of truth, so can we. Those who receive God as Father, Christ as Lord, and the Holy Spirit as Helper come to know His divine attributes.

In God's many expressions, titles, and names His character is revealed. To name a few, we can come to know God as "Adonai"—the Boss; "Christ"—the Redeemer; "Paraclete"—the Holy Spirit, Teacher, and Comforter; "Jesus"—the Way, the Truth, and the Life; and "Abba"—God, our heavenly Father through Christ.

Also, we must ever be mindful that God is not a man. God is Spirit. In the Christian faith God is known as "He" as we receive Him as our Abba (Father). In His earthly life Jesus Christ was God in the body of a human male. The Holy Spirit is also often referenced as "He." Yet please don't be turned away from God because of these masculine references. The Bible makes it clear:

> God is not a man, so he does not lie. He is not human, so he does not change his mind. Has he ever spoken and failed to act? Has he ever promised and not carried it through?
> —NUMBERS 23:19

> For God is Spirit, so those who worship him must worship in spirit and in truth.
> —JOHN 4:24

Those who receive God as Abba in the fullness of His loving grace through the shed blood of Jesus the Christ not only are God's creations, but they also become children of God. I believe it is the nature of the created to desire to worship the Creator.

We can begin to understand true worship by observing little children. For example, when my children were young, they were spontaneous worshippers. Today my precious grandchildren sing praise-and-worship songs spontaneously. There is something about the life and heart of an innocent child that can spring instantly into praise and worship, especially when surrounded by worshippers.

MORE THAN A SONG—DEVELOPING A HEART OF WORSHIP

After seeking to understand true godly worship, I now realize that while I may have been familiar with expressions of worship from childhood, I didn't have a heart or life of worship until I was born again in 1983. Yes, you may say, "But Alveda, you were a preacher's kid."

Well, being the child and grandchild of preachers won't save you. Salvation is a personal experience that precedes being able to experience the "in spirit and in truth" worship that Jesus spoke of to the woman at the well in John 4.

In the chapter on the divine key of salvation I spoke of my born-again experience and my early church days after that. It was at Fellowship of Faith Christian Church that songs such as "Joy of My Desire," "Give Thanks," "The Spirit Song," and so many other now-classic Christian songs became part of my budding worship experience.

As much as I cherished and still remember those beautiful days of deliverance and infilling at Fellowship of Faith with Pastor Wayne and Sister Gerri Thompson, I eventually was guided to leave them and go to another church, Believers' Bible Christian Church. When I walked through the door of BBCC in 1987, the senior pastor, Allen McNair, was greeting the congregation with these endearing words: "Welcome home." I was truly home, as I was first drawn to the music from the worship team.

Over the next few years I was blessed with the opportunity to grow spiritually, to write some Christian songs myself, and to become part of the church's music ministry. It was at BBCC that I learned from Pastor McNair that worship is more than a song.

Again, Jesus declared:

> But the time is coming—indeed it's here now—when true worshipers will worship the Father in spirit and in truth. The Father is looking for those who will worship him that way.
>
> —JOHN 4:23

It was during these early years at BBCC that I was introduced to worship leaders and songwriters, and I began to see the connection between living for Christ, obeying God's Word, and allowing those expressions to become part of the musical gifts and talents some people use to glorify God in the earth. Notice I say that "some people" use their musical gifts to glorify God. Everyone doesn't.

Among those who became my worship music mentors from a distance were Ron Kenoly, Kent Henry, Larnelle Harris, Sandi Patty, and LaMar Boschman. Of course there were many others. For years I was hungry for the sound of worship. I didn't realize the day would come when I would want to go deeper, to find the heart of worship.

As late as 2015, thirty-three years after being born again, I was still seeking the sound of David. I had asked God to take me to that place from which David the psalmist played and worshipped. Even though I knew by then that worship is more than a song, I was still looking for that portal-opening sound that would allow the angels to ascend and descend.

Somehow I found a website for Wholetones, a project that explores the healing musical frequencies found in David's psalms. I bought the book and CD and actually reached the developer, Michael S. Tyrrell, in person. Yet around this time, as I was seeking to discover that portal-opening sound, God reminded me that I would fall short of experiencing worship in spirit and in truth if I attempted to release the sound of worship without a heartfelt connection to Him, which includes obedience.

I was searching for David's key to worship; I was searching for true worship and divine frequencies in the worship experience. But in my seeking I began to understand that while godly worship music does play an integral role in bringing deliverance to tormented souls, music in itself cannot be the end-all of worship. Why? Because music can be used to bring good or evil to situations.

The Bible reveals that as David played, King Saul found relief from tormenting spirits. Yet we know that the music in and of itself only calmed King Saul's tormented soul. The music didn't deliver the king from torment because in the end he didn't find solace in true worship.

David was the true worshipper. He was more than a talented musician, gifted songwriter, and spontaneous dancer. Yes, David wrote many psalms and played the harp well. But there was more to David. Beyond his talents was his heart for worship.

Consider the reasons the following verse says David was recommended to play for Saul when the king was looking for a psalmist whose music could help relieve him of the torment he experienced.

> One of the servants answered, "I have seen a *son of Jesse* of Bethlehem who *knows how to play the lyre*. He is a *brave man* and *a warrior*. He *speaks well* and is *a fine-looking man*. And *the Lord is with him*."
> —1 SAMUEL 16:18, NIV, EMPHASIS ADDED

David was a skillful musician. That would have been a must for King Saul to invite David to play for him. But David also turned out to be a mighty man of valor. He was prudent in speech, handsome, and most importantly the Lord was with David.

Though music was what introduced David to King Saul, David's calling went far beyond his musical anointing. David's character may have been expressed in his music, but it was not defined by his music. David's character was more clearly defined in his roles as a son of Jesse, brave warrior, and prudent king. Yet what stood out most was the anointing on his life, evident by the fact that people said the Lord was with him.

Now, before we get into David's human failings and try to discredit him as a true worshipper, let's remember Psalm 51. After he sinned with Bathsheba, David repented and prayed for a clean heart. Later God affirmed David as a man after His own heart (Acts 13:22). Worship was a lifestyle for David, and the same should be true of us since worship is a key that unlocks our spiritual gifts.

I like what Dean Mitchum, worship leader at Vision Church at Christian International, says we can learn from David's example. In a blog post circulated through *The Elijah List*, Mitchum noted that of the seven attributes used to describe David in 1 Samuel 16:18, four related to David's character, and only one each addressed his talent, appearance, and anointing. Recognizing that, Mitchum had this to say to those called to be psalmists: "Build your prophetic reputation by not only being anointed and prophetic but also by building your character as well."[2]

Not everyone will lead others in worship in a church setting, but we are all called to build our character as we develop a lifestyle of worship. Over the years, my character and subsequent worship lifestyle have been strengthened through simple acts of obedience to God's Word, such as reading the Bible and applying its truths in my life. I also have been blessed to be part of a prophetic ministry at my church since 1987. In the early years, when Pastor McNair was writing and producing music with our music department head, I was honored to sing background in some of their studio sessions. As I have humbled myself to serve and learn, I have received prophetic downloads that have inspired me to write blogs, poetry, books, and songs such as "For the Lord Is Here," "Love Will Live," and "Latter Rain."

In Pastor McNair's latter years at BBCC, before his transition to heaven, I was tremendously blessed to join him in producing a "spiritual song" that came forth during one midweek service as he was ministering. After that service I went to my pastor and told him the song needed to be recorded. I remember his words. "You record it. Just make sure you sing it." So another song, "Heaven Comes to Me," was born.

Today as an evangelist, singer, and songwriter, I am blessed to be part of the BBCC music ministry and to lead praise and worship around the world. In these times of praise and worship I am not always singing with musical accompaniment.

In fact, one evening when I was singing with the music ministry at BBCC, a guest evangelist was leading worship. Under the unction of the Holy Spirit, he stopped singing, signaled for the musicians to stop playing, and said: "Use your words to express your devotion to our God. Not your song, not your talent, your words. Stop singing and playing, and talk to God. Express your love and willingness to serve our Master as you are speaking and professing your words to Him."

It was something else to shift right there on the platform from rehearsed singing and playing to speaking to Abba! The congregation quickly joined in, and we had a glorious time together in the holy presence of God!

As Jesus told His disciples, "God is a Spirit: and they that worship him must worship him in spirit and in truth" (John 4:24, KJV). True worship cannot be taught; it must be sought. As we study and apply the Word of God, we grow in His grace and find the path to true worship. Choose to be remembered as David was; he was not only "the sweet psalmist of Israel" (2 Sam. 23:1) and a prophet

(Acts 2:30), but God declared that he was a man after His own heart—a true son.

SCRIPTURE REFLECTION

David, the son of Jesse, speaks—David, the man who was raised up so high, David, the man anointed by the God of Jacob, David, the sweet psalmist of Israel. The Spirit of the LORD speaks through me; his words are upon my tongue.

—2 SAMUEL 23:1–2

PERSONAL REFLECTION

How can you improve genuine praise and true worship practices in your daily life?

PRAYER

Father, in the name of Jesus, teach me to live the life of praise as Your true worshipper. I pray this in Jesus's name by the power of Your Holy Spirit. Amen.

Chapter 13

DIVINE PROPHECY

Let love be your highest goal! But you should also desire the special abilities the Spirit gives—especially the ability to prophesy.

—1 CORINTHIANS 14:1

WHILE THIS DISCUSSION about prophecy may be one of the shorter chapters in this book, prophecy is in no way a minor divine key. In a ranking of importance, prophecy may belong right next to divine love on your spiritual key ring. First Corinthians 14:1 tells us that love is the most important force in the universe and beyond. Yet the spiritual gift that is listed right after love is prophecy. So it is faith, hope, love, and now prophecy abiding together on the divine key ring that allow us to walk in our full purpose and potential in God.

Prophecy is "something that is declared by a prophet, especially a divinely inspired prediction, instruction, or exhortation."[1] The Bible has much to say about this key. From a biblical perspective we are urged to honor God's genuine prophets and shun false prophets. Yet while prophecy is important, 1 Corinthians reminds us that if we possess and master all the spiritual gifts, including the great prophetic gift, without the master key— divine love—we are making useless noise.

In previous chapters I have shared many personal testimonies of how I've applied the various divine spiritual keys in my spiritual journey. In this chapter I want to briefly share some of the prophetic words and encounters that have shaped my life. While I make short mention of them here, several of these experiences are discussed more fully in other chapters.

WHERE MY PROPHETIC EDGE WAS SHARPENED

Often when speaking or journaling in my blog or on social media, I discuss my family ties. As the niece of the famous Dr. Martin Luther King Jr., I quote passages from his "I Have a Dream" speech from time to time. Then when I share that I too have a dream, people assume Uncle ML's speech is the frame of reference for my dream. This just isn't the case.

My dream stems from the dream my paternal grandfather had before I was born, where he saw me and was able to describe me to my mother with perfect accuracy. (There was no ultrasound in those days.) My mother considered aborting me, so Granddaddy's prophetic dream saved my life.

My longtime pastor, Allen McNair, was a prophetic voice who spoke into my life for nearly thirty years. It was Pastor McNair, speaking from God's heart, who guided me into my Queen Esther call. He directed me to step away from politics, accept the mantle of evangelist, and form King for America, now Alveda King Ministries, which has served the United States and the world since 1998.

Through the years Pastor McNair spoke wisdom and healing over and into my life for health, relationships, and ministry. Many times, by the laying on of hands, Pastor McNair imparted to me the anointing for the mantle and gifts operating in his life. I would often chuckle and say my name could have been "Elishaette" or "Timothia" because I was truly being mentored by a great man of God. I am forever grateful that God placed me into the ministry of Pastor Allen McNair.

I further received the prophetic mantles of liturgical songwriting, singing, dancing, banner ministry, and poetry from several prophetic voices, including Pastor McNair. At BBCC I developed a hunger and thirst for the varied prophetic worship expressions. Launching out "into the deep," I learned from guest prophets and ministries who came to BBCC, such as Lori Wilke of Spirit to Spirit Ministry in Milwaukee, Wisconsin.

I have also studied under other prophetic ministries around the world, such as those of Myles Munroe, Billy Graham, Darryl Winston, LaMar Boschman, Kent Henry (where I began to understand and experience spiritual portals opening and God's holy angels ascending and descending), Jimmy Swaggart, Morris Cerullo, Hosanna! and Integrity Music, Gwen Shaw, T. D. Jakes, The Elijah List, *Charisma* magazine, Charlotte Baker, Rita Springer, and so many more. I received formal prophetic training from various schools of ministry, including that of BBCC, Kenneth Hagin, and Life Center Ministries.

After the titles and roles of mother and grandmother, I honor the title of evangelist most because this is God's assignment that my beloved Pastor McNair prophesied I would walk in not long before he left this earth. It is a call I take seriously.

A LEGACY OF PROPHETIC GIFTS

I also have a prophetic mantle that is part of the King family legacy. My siblings, children, grandchildren, cousins, and I each have evidence of the prophetic gift in our lives. We are often noted as seers and visionaries, with several of us having the gift of dreams and interpretation of dreams. Those who have gone on before us—Daddy, Granddaddy, Uncle ML, and so many others—shared their prophetic gifts on this earth.

In the 1990s Pastor McNair said to me, "You have an end-time ministry. You must prepare." Pastor gave me several books to read, and I began to explore the prophetic nature of ministry more deeply. During his lifetime Pastor McNair was an apostle, prophet, teacher, and pastor. I have done my best to follow his Christian example and teachings as he followed Christ our Savior.

Perhaps you have some evidence of a prophetic gift working in your life. Being able to hear from God is essential to reaching your spiritual potential. One who hears God and does what He says receives the benefits of blessing, favor, opportunity, and promotion to greater things. I encourage you to find a prophetic mentor, one who is humble, is not intimidated by your gifts, and will always point you to Jesus.

I also encourage you to stir up the gifts of God that are inside of you through some of the other keys we've mentioned so far, namely prayer, worship, and Bible study. Let the Word of God become like your daily food. Jesus said man does "not live by bread alone, but by every word that comes from the mouth of God" (Matt. 4:4). I also encourage you to get knowledge, wisdom, and understanding about your prophetic gift through books and other resources created by those who have excelled in this gift.

The prophetic gift plays such a critical role in advancing the kingdom of God and its principles. The civil rights movement of the 1960s would not have been what it was had it not been for the prophetic nature of the men and women who led it. Prophecy allows you to see what God sees. Prophecy allows you into the presence of God to know His secret thoughts and plans for the future. He shares these secrets with His servants to build faith and expectation among the people of God so they can press toward something greater. This is the potential of the gift of God burning in your soul. I challenge you to pursue it and see how God will change your life and those around you.

KING FAMILY TRUTH

"When God speaks, who can but prophesy?"[2]
—Martin Luther King Jr., quoting Amos 3:8

In closing I'd like to share a prophetic parable by Charlotte Baker I first heard at a meeting hosted by worship leader Kent Henry in the 1980s. This word from God continues to resonate in my life today. I pray it will bless you too.

THE EYE OF THE NEEDLE PROPHECY

I stood among the sons of men, strong and tall. My heart was filled with enthusiasm. My life was given to the purpose of God. Upon that day, I said to the Lord, "I will do mighty exploits in the name of my God."

The Lord came unto me, and He said, "What is it, son of man, that thou wouldst have?"

I said, "Lord, if I would only be among those who play sweetly upon an instrument and who sing well in the house of the Lord, then I would do great things for my God."

The Lord came to me, and He gave unto me the desire of my heart. He stood me among the sons of men. He let me play, and He let me sing. I saw the day when the hearts of men were moved by that thing that the Lord had given unto me.

After hearts of men were moved, I stood back, and I said to myself, "Now I will be content, for I have been able to move the hearts of men." But in my secret hour, I bowed my heart before my God and said, "Lord, Thou hast given what I asked for, but my heart is heavy. I have a longing for something more."

He came again unto me in the night season. He asked me again, "Son of man, ask Me again the thing that thou wouldst have of Me."

I said, "Lord, I see men bowed by burdens low. I see hearts that are broken. I see sadness and discouragement. O, give me the power of the spoken word that I might speak the Word and their hearts will be delivered."

The Lord came unto me and said, "Son of man, I have given thee the things which thou has desired."

With great joy, I marched before the people of God. In my youth and in my enthusiasm, I spoke the Word and men were delivered. I spoke the Word, and their hearts were made whole. I know what it was to bind the brokenhearted and to pour in the oil of joy for mourning.

While men were praising Him and glorifying His name, I went back to my secret chamber. I bowed my head in sorrow. I said, "O my God, O my God. I am not satisfied."

He came again unto me and He said, "Son of man, what is it that thou again desirest of Me?"

And I said, "O my God, give me power in my hands that as Thou didst do, I might lay my hands upon the sick and see healing flow."

He said unto me, "It is done as thou has commanded."

From that very day, as I went to the nations of the Earth, I saw the sick raised from their sick beds. I saw pain and suffering go away.

I was rejoicing as I went to my secret place. I bowed my head before my God. I said, "Now, my God, I will be satisfied, for Thou has given me that which I have desired."

No sooner had the words come out of my mouth when the heart within me began to ache and cry. I said, "God, I do not understand this. Again my heart is sad." I said, "Lord, wilt Thou just one more time give me the thing I ask of Thee?"

He said, "It is done."

I said, "God, I desire to go against principalities and powers, the powers of the wickedness of this world in spiritual darkness in high places."

He said, "Surely I give it unto thee. Now go."

So I went, and the Lord allowed me to go into dens of iniquity and holes and dives where men hide from the light because of the sin and evil that is upon them. There was a day when I saw demons cry out at the very presence of the power of God that rested.

Then I went back to my secret place broken. I said, "God, I have asked Thee for all that I desire, and still my heart is not satisfied. Nor do I feel that I have touched the thing that Thou hast called me to. In my youth I had expended myself with all the things that my heart had desired." Then one more time a gracious and loving God visited me in the night season. He said, "Now, what is it that thou dost desire?"

In brokenness of heart, I bowed before Him, and I said, "God, only that thing which Thou dost desire to give unto me."

He came unto me and said, "Come with Me, and I will take thee on a journey." He took me past my friends. He took me past those with whom I had come into the house of the Lord. He took me into a desolate place. He caused me to go into a place alone in the wilderness.

I said, "O my God, Thou hast cut me off from those I love. What art Thou doing unto me?"

He said, "I take thee to the place where all men must come if their heart's cry is to be fulfilled."

At a certain hour, I bowed before a gate that is called, "the Eye of the Needle." There before the Eye of the Needle I heard the voice of the Lord say, "Bow low." I bowed low. He said, "No, lower." So I bowed lower. He said, "Yet lower. Thou dost not go low enough." So I went as low as I could go.

I had upon my back my books of learning. I had with me my instruments of music. I had with me my gifts and abilities. He said unto me, "Thou hast too much, thou canst not go through this gate."

I said, "God, Thou hast given me these books. Thou hast given me these abilities."

He said, "Drop them, or thou dost not go." So I dropped them, and I went on through a very small gate that is called "the Eye of the Needle."

As I went through this gate, I heard the voice of the Lord say, "Now rise to the other side." As I rose, a very strange thing happened to me. For lo, the gate which was so small that I must lay aside everything, was so wide I could not fill it.

As I stood in the presence of the Lord, I said, "God, what is this thing that Thou hast done unto me, for my soul is now satisfied?"

He said, "Thou hast come through the gate of worship. Now come up to the Circle of the Earth, and I will show thee a great mystery. I will reveal unto thee the thing that I am doing among the sons of men."

The Spirit of the Lord caught me away. He took me to the Circle of the Earth, higher than the eagle flies, beyond where the clouds can rumble, beyond where the sun shines or the moon finds her path. There at the throne of my God, He said, "Look down upon My people."

I saw strange things. I saw my compassions gathered around a very small gate. I saw them wringing their hands and crying. They were saying to one another, "God hath given us these instruments of war. This sword is my sword, and I will work against the enemy. I will bring the enemy down. I cannot go through this gate, for if I go through this gate, I must put down my sword. God had called me to be a warrior, and therefore I will not do it."

And I heard another one say, "Me? Lay down my instruments of music? Lay down all that God has given unto me, just to go through that silly little gate, to be nothing but a bare man who comes out on the other side stripped of everything? I cannot do this thing!" I saw them as they stood aside in their pride, afraid to bow themselves before a very small gate.

Then I saw again, as the Lord brought me closer to the gate, I saw a man bow low, laying down everything that he had. As he came through the very wide gate on the other side, his instruments of music were there. His sword was there. His books were there. The power was there.

The word of the Lord came to me, "Go now and tell this people before thee, I have given unto this people extreme talents and much ability. I have called those who are instrumentalists to play. But I say unto thee this day, if thou dost not come through the very small gate, which is the gate of worship, and bow low and lay before Me thine instruments, thy talents, thine abilities, thy vision, and the power, thou shalt always be among those who will only be able to minister to the hearts of men and bless the hearts of men.

But there is a gate open in the Church in this hour which is a very small gate. Through that gate only men who are worshippers will go. These men will lay talents before their God. These men will say, "God, we will be worshippers." Through that wide gate they will come. As they come through that wide gate (hear again the Word of the Lord), they will arise again on the other side, not to minister unto men, but to minister unto their God.

I now present before thee a choice. Thou canst minister unto men, and I will cause thee to sway the hearts of men with thy talent. Or thou canst humble thyself as one passing through a very low gate and become a worshiper of God. Then thou shalt minister unto the King.[3]

This, the best known of her prophetic parables, was given by Baker at the 1981 National Worship Symposium in Dallas, Texas. It reveals to us God's plan for us to excel in our gifts and use them to bless and minister to people. The Lord has given us the authority and power to operate in the gifts He has given us. It is through His revealed Word that we are able to learn how He wants us to use these gifts to their fullest potential. When we petition Him to speak His will over our lives, we activate the prophetic realm.

It is His desire to grant us the desire that He has placed in our hearts. The Bible says we are to call out to Him and He will show us great and mighty things that we do not know. This is the power of divine prophecy, without which we cannot live up to our potential.

SCRIPTURE REFLECTION

Surely the Sovereign LORD does nothing without revealing his plan to his servants the prophets.

—AMOS 3:7, NIV

PERSONAL REFLECTION

How can the gift of prophecy be used in or applied to your life?

PRAYER

Lord, Your Word teaches that prophecy is a gift to be desired. Help me understand Your heart for prophecy in today's world. In Jesus's name I pray. Amen.

Chapter 14

DIVINE UNDERSTANDING

This I say therefore, and testify in the Lord, that ye henceforth walk not as other Gentiles walk, in the vanity of their mind, having the understanding darkened, being alienated from the life of God through the ignorance that is in them, because of the blindness of their heart.... And be renewed in the spirit of your mind.

—EPHESIANS 4:17–18, 23, KJV

As I HAVE said throughout our journey, music has played a critical role in my spiritual experience. It has helped me to enter into worship and to hear the Spirit of God speak to me Spirit to spirit and convict my heart. In particular, the songs "Be Magnified," as sung by Kent Henry, and Richard Smallwood's rendition of "Center of My Joy" illuminated my understanding of the connection between obedience, submission, and worship. These songs helped me realize that God must be at the center of everything, and in recognizing that, I was able to really focus on Him and develop a more intimate relationship with Him. When I gave God my undivided attention, I began to understand His Word on a deeper level.

Even today, if I allow myself to get too far away from the Word—if I skip a day of Bible reading and quiet time—I find myself wrestling with confusion as I juggle the tasks of the day. It's amazing that my children and now even their children can tell when I haven't spent time with God. As things begin to spiral out of control, either slowly or rapidly, often one of my adult children will ask, "Mom, have you prayed today? Please go take a prayer break."

During my prayer times I read the Bible, listen to inspirational music, pray, and sit quietly before the Lord. It is during these times that God teaches me, heals me, and blesses me with His holy companionship. Revelation often floods into my understanding with such intensity that my human brain can hardly contain it all.

Proverbs 4:5 teaches, "Get wisdom, get understanding: forget it not; neither decline from the words of my mouth" (KJV). As we seek to know God's plan for our lives, we come to understand our purpose. I marvel at the understanding that comes from being alone with God and in His Word. Often as I read the Word, I find myself thinking, "I've read this passage many times. Why didn't I see this before?," or "I've heard this song so many times.

Why am I just getting this now?" It's amazing how much we can learn just by spending time alone with God.

Some people feel as if they cannot have special times with God during their regular, everyday routines. They think super spiritual encounters with God only occur in special places at special times, but that is not so. It is important to develop a daily discipline of worship and prayer. You don't have to be in a prayer closet or an especially quiet place to hear from God. You and God can be alone even in a crowded room.

I've often said that Satan wants us to buy the lie that we can only pray in special places. If people have to wait to get home or to church or to their prayer closets, they are fair game for the devil's attacks when they are outside of those sacred zones they have set up. Psalm 91 is the real sacred zone. We can hide in the secret place of the most high God anywhere and anytime, whether we are alone or in a crowd; praying without ceasing means praying all the time, anywhere. We must learn to pray, to praise, and to give thanksgiving to God at all times, everywhere.

No matter where we are, God has a way of arresting our hearts if we remain open and surrendered to Him. By staying in a posture where our hearts are saying, "Yes, God," we keep ourselves available to hear from Him at any time, in any place, and under any circumstance. Making ourselves available to God in this way will help us learn His nature, communicate with Him, and know His will for our lives.

When we understand how to function within God's will and thereby obey God's promptings and leadings, we become much more effective as ambassadors of His kingdom here on earth. As we grow in our relationship with God, we begin to see great and miraculous things happen in our lives and in the lives of people we pray for and mentor. This is not reserved for leaders; it's for all people. God wants every believer to seek out answers to the questions about our purpose that are deep in our hearts. God doesn't just speak to leaders about these things. He isn't a respecter of persons.

In my earlier days as a born-again Christian I had so many questions in my heart and mind. Pastors, church leaders, and Christian TV personalities didn't seem to have the answers I sought. So I learned to seek God for truth. Scriptures such as, "Ye have not, because ye ask not" (James 4:2, KJV), and "Ask, and it shall be given you; seek, and ye shall find; knock, and it shall be opened unto you" (Matt. 7:7, KJV) resonated in my heart and mind as I dared to ask God about almost any- and everything.

One of the deepest issues I've wrestled with is related to my identity. Through the years it has been a big challenge for me to walk confidently in my own skin as a black Christian woman, so I asked God to show me who I really am. God has responded to that request, and He has shown me things regarding the journey toward the liberation of black people, a journey closely aligned with my call as a guardian of the King family legacy, that are not addressed in most churches.

"People of color" have experienced a lot of hurt through the years. Because the world has bought the lie of "separate races," all too often we as blacks have felt disenfranchised, and we have somehow become a nation within a nation. Through my journey, God revealed a special message to me about this issue, which He inspired me to write in my book *Who We Are in Christ Jesus*. Due to unfair treatment people of color may sometimes feel they are not as valuable as other people, and this feeling doesn't automatically disappear just because they go to church. When we seek healing from God and answers about His special plan for us, the truth He reveals often brings confidence and a flood of love and worth into our hearts.

God opened the door to understanding for me as I sought to know Him and trusted Him for answers to my questions about His thoughts toward me. If you are reading this and you have ever felt the weight of racial injustice or have struggled with relating and ministering to people who have experienced hurt in this area, I pray these revelations help you understand how all of our purposes are intertwined for the expansion of God's kingdom.

UNDERSTANDING MY IDENTITY IN CHRIST[1]

According to biblical history, all human life, springing from Adam and Eve, began in Eden. Adam and Eve had dominion in the Garden of Eden, which was bordered by the Pishon and Gihon rivers. Although there isn't universal consensus on which rivers these are, because of the scholarship of John L. Johnson, author of *The Black Biblical Heritage*, I believe these are the Blue Nile and White Nile rivers, which are located in Africa.

This leads me to believe Adam and Eve and their children populated Earth from Africa and lived there for many years. On this point there is much agreement. A 1987 study published in the journal *Nature* found that all living females descend from a single maternal ancestor and that she was African.[2] Other studies also claim mankind originated in Africa and ultimately migrated from there to other parts of the world.[3] The fact that mankind can trace our roots to Africa has caused some scientists to deduce that Adam and Eve were "black." Others, however, believe Eve and her descendants may have been "red skinned," deriving their hue from the color of the soil in the region where they may have lived.[4] Whatever the case, Adam and Eve were likely "people of color," as were their children.

Several generations after Adam and Eve, the earth was drenched by a fierce flood, destroying life as it was, with the exception of Noah and his family and a selection of animals, who were preserved in the ark. Noah, a man who faithfully served God, had three sons—Shem, Ham, and Japheth—who left the ark after it rested on Mount Ararat when the floodwaters receded.

Shem, Ham, and Japheth and their wives survived the flood to repopulate the earth. The descendants of Japheth included the people in Europe, thus composing what we think of as the "white" people.[5] The sons of Ham spread into Asia and Northern Africa, and the descendants of Shem largely occupied the Middle East.[6]

Some Christian scientists believe Noah and his wife had medium-brown skin and that their offspring carried DNA that allowed them to produce children of both lighter and darker skin tones. As Shem, Ham, Japheth, and their descendants spread to various parts of the world, certain groups lost the ability to produce children of different shades because the genetic information to produce those skin tones eventually was lost after several generations.[7] The environments into which the groups settled also influenced their skin color and features.[8] For instance, as the sons of Japheth moved into what is now considered Europe, their bodies began to produce less melanin, and their skin became "white."

Based on Johnson's research, I believe Shem was a dark-skinned man and that Abram, who was born about two hundred years after the flood, was also dark-skinned. Abram lived in Ur until God sent him forth into his destiny. According to Johnson, during Abram's day, the natives of Ur of Chaldea were a deep-black-skinned people.[9] If you know the story in Genesis, God called Abram to leave his people and ultimately changed his name to Abraham. With his wife, Sarah, Abraham became the father of Isaac, who became the father of Israel (known as Jacob before God changed his name).

Before Israel was born, God told Abram, "Thy seed shall be a stranger in a land that is not theirs, and shall serve them; and they shall afflict them four hundred years" (Gen. 15:13, KJV). God also promised to judge that nation and send the seed out of bondage with great substance (v. 14). This was a prophecy and a promise that was fulfilled when the children of Israel left Egypt as captives.

Generations later Solomon was born to Israel's King David, who descended from the union of Salmon and Rahab, a woman many believe was black.[10] King Solomon had many wives of color. Some believe one of them was the Ethiopian queen of Sheba and that she bore Solomon a son named Menelik I, who allegedly became an emperor in Ethiopia.[11] Menelik I is credited as the father of the Falasha Jews, also called Beta Israel. The Falasha claim Solomon ordered over twelve thousand members from each tribe of Israel to assist Menelik's journey back to Africa following a visit to his father. This multitude intermingled with the people of Ethiopia and became known as the Falasha Jews.[12] In recent decades the Falasha returned home to Israel in the care and company of their Israeli brothers, which fulfilled the Bible prophecy that the Jewish people would return to Israel.[13]

The Falasha were not the only Jewish people in Africa. Through the centuries the Jewish people have faced persecution from various nations—from Rome in the first century AD on to Nazi Germany during the twentieth century. To escape oppression, the Jewish people fled throughout the world, with many settling in Africa.[14] As those Jewish refugees lived among the Hamitic people of Africa, I believe they intermarried with them yet maintained their heritage. In recent years scientists have begun to confirm this. For instance, DNA studies have shown that male members of the Lemba people, a black African tribe in Zimbabwe, carry the genes of the Cohanim, a priestly caste of ancient Jews. Interestingly the Lemba also practice several customs that resemble those of ancient Hebrews.[15]

It is likely that some of the black Jews in Africa were sold as slaves to the Americas and continued to "sing the Lord's songs in a strange land." This leads me to believe that American blacks descend from all three of Noah's sons, giving us a rich heritage. We have the blood of all three brothers in one body and thus encompass the whole family of mankind.

It has been life-changing for me to realize that having black skin is not a curse, as some have said through the years, but is part of God's good plan for my life. Gaining this understanding has allowed me to see myself as God sees me—as His beloved child, made in His image and heir to the covenant He made with Abraham.

KING FAMILY TRUTH

God sees us all as His beloved children, made in His image.

Will slavery, segregation, and racism be abolished in America by the year 2019? As we approach the four hundredth anniversary of the beginning of slavery in America, I can't help but wonder if America will finally repent of the sin of racism and accept that God created humans as one blood. Rather than wax prophetic as I did in previous writings, I'm going to just pray and trust God for the transformation that will bring healing to our nation and to our land.

Let us move ahead with the faith that God's promise in Genesis 15:14 to send His people out of bondage with great substance could be fulfilled again in our day. Though slavery in the United States officially ended in 1865 with the ratification of the Thirteenth Amendment, oppression of minorities still continues in various forms. I believe we are on the verge of breaking the yoke of racism here in the twenty-first century. As we accept the truth that racism is a sin and that human beings are created as the "one blood" family that God intends, racism can die and agape love can rise up.

ASK GOD FOR UNDERSTANDING OF HIS WILL FOR YOUR LIFE

It has been years since I began to seek God for answers to Bible puzzles, social dilemmas, family problems, my identity in Him, and so much more. As I have sought Him for answers, I have come to recognize the importance of daily Bible reading. This practice, which has been a part of my daily regimen for more than three decades, has given me insights that have inspired many of my blogs, interview responses, books, and sermons.

In Jeremiah 33:3 God says, "Call to Me and I will answer you and show you great and mighty things…, which you do not know" (AMPC). Psalm 119:144 says, "The righteousness of Your testimonies is everlasting; give me understanding, and I shall live" (NKJV). Understanding is tied to life, and if I may say so, abundant life. You need understanding to walk confidently in your purpose, and God is excited about giving it to you.

There are many things in life that can leave you feeling confused about who you are, just as some things in my cultural history affected me in that way. But God is a restorer. Jesus has returned to us—His joint heirs—the keys to the kingdom, which include being able to understand the will of God for our lives. We have the authority to stop the effects of sin and injustice and be healed.

Though I spent time here talking about what God revealed to me about my ethnic history, God loves all the people of the world with a great and everlasting love. He desires to tell us the secrets of His amazing plans and purposes for our lives. You do not have to walk in confusion, believing the lies of the enemy. Seek understanding, and pursue His truth, which is revealed as we communicate with God in prayer and by meditating on His Word. When we fight our way through the hindrances that rob us of the time to know and understand God, we gain victory over ignorance as understanding is imparted.

SCRIPTURE REFLECTION

For we are not fighting against flesh-and-blood enemies,
but against evil rulers and authorities of the unseen world,

against mighty powers in this dark world, and against evil spirits in the heavenly places.

—EPHESIANS 6:12

PERSONAL REFLECTION

Are there any spiritual disciplines you need to apply so you can better understand God's purpose for your life? If so, which ones? Do you believe you have misunderstood what it means to live for Him? If so, how?

PRAYER

Dear heavenly Father, Your Word teaches me that if I need wisdom, I should ask of You. Help me understand You more. Reveal to me the hopeful and prosperous plans You have for my future. In Jesus's name I pray. Amen.

Official White House photo by Shealah Craighead

President Donald J. Trump gave me a big hug after we toured the Smithsonian's National Museum of African American History and Culture in February 2017. I could tell he was moved as we explored the exhibits that show how far God has brought African Americans—from slave ships to the highest levels of leadership in this nation.

Chapter 15

DIVINE LIFE

And hath made of one blood all nations of men
for to dwell on all the face of the earth.

—ACTS 17:26, KJV

Jesus said, "I came that they may have life and have it abundantly" (John 10:10, ESV). To God, our lives are of the highest value. He sent His only Son into the world to die for us, even while we were sinning against Him. He has plans for our lives that exceed our thoughts and expectations (Eph. 3:20).

Yet with all that He has planned for us when we decide to follow Him, He still gives us the opportunity to choose between life and death. Deuteronomy 30:19 says, "Today I have given you the choice between life and death, between blessings and curses. Now I call on heaven and earth to witness the choice you make. Oh, that you would choose life, so that you and your descendants might live!" Our Father urges us to choose life, not only for ourselves but also for generations to come.

Race and justice have been themes throughout this book. Both themes relate to God's ultimate plan for us as we are created in His image. Whether black, white, Hispanic, Asian, or another ethnic group, all people—from the day we are conceived until the day we die—matter to God. This is a truth that motivated my family and many others in the fight for racial justice and equality. Racism opposes God's gift of life by causing people of one ethnic group to fight for supremacy and deny those of another ethnicity the same quality of life they enjoy.

Having come to know God's love for us and the life He blesses us with, I have taken on another fight for justice, as you may already know—the fight for the right to life for unborn babies. I'd like to talk about how violating God's love for us in this area can have serious effects on our ability to reach our full potential and live out our purposes.

THE RIGHT TO LIFE

During the twentieth century the door was opened to invade the wombs of mothers, the stability of the family, the sanctity of marriage, and the sacredness of the human personality. In the name of civil rights, abortion was legalized by the Supreme Court ruling in the 1973 *Roe v. Wade* case. Since then more than fifty-nine million babies have been legally aborted in the United States.[1] Currently roughly one-third of the babies aborted are African American.[2] Sadly two of those aborted babies are mine. As I reflect on the reality of black genocide that has loomed over the African American community since the days of slavery in this nation, I find that the dream of Martin Luther King Jr. is continually threatened by the abortion of our children and the injury to the wombs and health of their mothers.

Films such as *Maafa 21, Blood Money,* and others provide evidence of a continuing pattern of genocide and eugenics—an idea that humanity could be improved through selective breeding—all rooted in the triple evils of racism, reproductive genocide, and sexual perversion—a three-headed monster. This pattern must be broken by the power of truth, which is the power of God. It is my prayer that my personal testimony will shed liberating truth on the issue of abortion that tramples the civil rights of our weakest, the children in the wombs of vulnerable mothers.

In a 1967 sermon my uncle ML preached that "man is a child of God, made in His image, and therefore must be respected as such....And when we truly believe in the sacredness of human personality, we won't exploit people, we won't trample over people with the iron feet of oppression, we won't kill anybody."[3]

In this great country of ours no one should be forced to pray or read any religious documents, and everyone should have the right to decide what to do with his or her own body. I remain amazed that the argument regarding this issue of body rights is often limited to the discussion of abortion in the twenty-first century. Human trafficking, slavery, and other oppressive ills that rob human beings of their body rights also are impacting our global society. For all of them, the bottom line is the same: we are overlooking the sanctity of all human life. Sadly too many are trying to deny the truth of God's Word, which teaches people about their God-given rights and how to enjoy them in full.

Thank God for the US Constitution. Our Constitution still guarantees freedom *of* religion and not freedom *from* religion, but the doctrine of separation of church and state is generally misappropriated and misinterpreted. Nothing in our constitution forbids the free exercise of religion in the public square. Trying to keep God out of government or any part of our existence is like trying to empty the ocean with a sieve. Inherent in our constitutional right to life, liberty, and the pursuit of happiness is the right to know the serious consequences of deciding to deny religious freedom or to abort our children.

If he were alive today, what would Uncle ML say? He dreamed of having his four children judged by the content of their characters, not just the color of their skin. What would he say if he'd lived to see the contents of thousands of children's skulls emptied into the bottomless caverns of abortionists' pits? What would he say about the rivers of blood from the children cut down in gang wars and other dark deeds?

It is time for America, perhaps the most blessed nation on earth, to lead the world in repentance and in restoration of life! If only we would carry the freedom of repentance to its fullest potential. If only America would seek to forgive and be forgiven, to repent and turn away from the sins of our nation. We must allow light and life back into our lives. This way, as God fans the fires of revival, we can see people turn away from death to life.

THE DAY I JOINED THE FIGHT FOR LIFE

Today I live with a repentant heart, and I pray in thanks each day for the Lord's forgiveness and blessing. I am a mother of six living children and a grandmother. Regrettully I am also a post-abortive mother. I offer a tearful prayer that sharing the tragedy of my life-altering experiences will help save the life of a child still unborn.

In the early 1970s, even though some black voices were protesting forced sterilization, artificial chemical birth control methods, and abortion, there were many who were fooled and misled by propaganda that promoted such strategies. I was among those who were duped. As a result, I suffered one involuntary and one voluntary legal abortion.

My involuntary abortion was performed just prior to the passage of *Roe v. Wade* by my private pro-abortion physician without my consent. I had gone to the doctor to ask why my cycle had not resumed after the birth of my son. I did not ask for and did not want an abortion. The doctor said, "You don't need to be pregnant. Let's see." He proceeded to perform a painful examination that resulted in a gush of blood and tissue emanating from my womb. He explained that he had performed an abortion called a local D and C.

Soon after the *Roe v. Wade* decision, I became pregnant again. There was adverse pressure and the threat of violence from the baby's father. The convenience provided through *Roe v. Wade* made it too easy for me to make the fateful decision to abort our child. I went to a Planned Parenthood–sanctioned doctor and was advised that the procedure would hurt no more than "having a tooth removed."

The next day, I was admitted to the hospital, and our baby was aborted. My medical insurance paid for the procedure. As soon as I woke up, I knew that something was very wrong. I felt very ill and empty. I tried to talk to the doctor and nurses about it. They assured me that the feelings would all go away in a few days. "You will be fine," they lied. And they are still lying today.

Planned Parenthood is America's number one provider of death by abortion. It has far-reaching tentacles into nations across the globe, promoting abortion worldwide. Planned Parenthood founder Margaret Sanger supported eugenics. In 1934 she even drafted a proposed law that included this provision: "Feeble-minded persons, habitual congenital criminals, those afflicted with inheritable disease, and others found biologically unfit by authorities qualified judge should be sterilized or, in cases of doubt, should be so isolated as to prevent the perpetuation of their afflictions by breeding." Sanger noted that she wanted "to give certain dysgenic groups in our population their choice of segregation or sterilization," which some have seen as a reference to concentration camps.[4]

In her quest to limit the number of those deemed "biologically unfit," Sanger founded an organization that has left in its wake nearly sixty million legal abortions in the United States from 1973 until the publishing date of this book. I am a victim of the deeds of Planned Parenthood.

Over the next few years after my abortions I experienced medical problems. I had trouble bonding with my son and his five siblings who were born after the abortions. I began to suffer from eating disorders, depression, nightmares, sexual dysfunctions, and a host of other issues related to the abortion I chose to have. I felt angry about both the involuntary and voluntary abortions and very guilty about the abortion I chose to have. The guilt made me very ill.

Like my uncle ML, who had received the Margaret Sanger Planned Parenthood Award in 1968, I became a victim to the lies of Planned Parenthood. They told my uncle, and they told me and millions of mothers and fathers, that their agenda was to help our people. They lied. Their agenda is deadly!

I pray often for deliverance from the pain caused by my decision to abort my baby. I suffered the threat of cervical and breast cancer and experienced the pain of empty arms after the baby was gone. Truly for me and countless post-abortive mothers nothing on earth can fully restore what has been lost—only Jesus can.

My children have all suffered from knowing that they have a brother or sister whom their mother chose to abort. Often they ask if I ever thought about aborting them, and they have said, "You killed our baby."

This is very painful for all of us. My mother and grandparents were very sad to know about the loss of the baby. The aborted child's father also regrets the abortions. If it had not been for *Roe v. Wade*, I would never have had that second abortion.

My birthday is January 22, and each year this special day is marred by the fact that it is also the anniversary of *Roe v. Wade*—and the anniversary of death for millions of babies. My deceased children and I are victims of abortion. The *Roe v. Wade* decision has adversely affected the lives of my entire family.

My grandfather Martin Luther King Sr. twice said, "No one is going to kill a child of mine." The first time Daddy King said this was to my mother, who was facing an "inconvenient pregnancy" with me. The next time he said it, I was facing a pregnancy. In both instances Daddy King said no and saved his seed.

KING FAMILY TRUTH

"No one is going to kill a child of mine."
—Martin Luther King Sr.

Tragically two of his grandchildren had already been aborted when he saved the life of his next great-grandson with this statement.

SAVING UNCLE ML'S DREAM

Any acts that chemically or surgically dismember and kill babies in the womb threaten the fabric of humanity. Butchering women under the falsehood of providing "safe abortions" hides the truth that many hysterectomies, breast cancer surgeries, and other female reproductive illnesses are the result of abortion.[5] They promote death over life in the name of abortion, and pro-choice people call it civil rights. But how can my uncle ML's dream survive if we murder our children?

Every aborted baby is like a slave in the womb of his or her mother. Whether the child lives or dies is in the hands of the mother—a decision empowered by *Roe v. Wade*. That choice, the final choice of whether the child lives or dies, should be left to God, who ultimately says, "Choose life!"

Mother Teresa said this:

> I feel that the greatest destroyer of peace today is abortion, because it is a war against the child—a direct killing of the innocent child—murder by the mother herself. And if we accept that a mother can kill even her own child, how can we tell other people not to kill one another? How do we persuade a woman not to have an abortion? As always, we must persuade her with love, and we remind ourselves that

love means to be willing to give until it hurts. Jesus gave even his life to love us. So the mother who is thinking of abortion, should be helped to love—that is, to give until it hurts her plans, or her free time, to respect the life of her child. The father of that child, whoever he is, must also give until it hurts. By abortion, the mother does not learn to love, but kills even her own child to solve her problems. And by abortion, the father is told that he does not have to take any responsibility at all for the child he has brought into the world. That father is likely to put other women into the same trouble. So abortion just leads to more abortion. Any country that accepts abortion is not teaching the people to love, but to use any violence to get what they want. That is why the greatest destroyer of love and peace is abortion.[6]

I join the voices of thousands across America who are silent no more. We can't sit idly by and allow this horrible spirit of murder to cut down—yes, cut out and cut away—our unborn and destroy the lives of our mothers. Our babies and our mothers must live! A woman has a right to choose what she does with her body, but the baby is not her body. Where is the lawyer for the baby? How can the dream survive if we murder our children?

I am very grateful to God for the spirit of repentance that is sweeping our land. In repentance there is healing. In the name of Jesus we must humble ourselves and pray, and turn from our wicked ways, so that God will hear from heaven and heal our land (2 Chron. 7:14).

KING FAMILY TRUTH

"The Negro cannot win as long as he is willing to sacrifice the futures of his children for immediate personal comfort and safety. Injustice anywhere is a threat to justice everywhere."[7]

—Martin Luther King Jr.

I, like my uncle, have a dream. I still have a dream that someday the men and women of our nation, the boys and girls of America, will come to our senses, humble ourselves before God Almighty, and receive His healing grace. I pray this is the day and hour of our deliverance. I pray that we will regain a commitment to life and finally obtain the promised liberty, justice, and pursuit of happiness for all. Let us end injustice anywhere by championing justice everywhere, including in the womb. May God, by His grace, have mercy on us all.

SCRIPTURE REFLECTION

Today I have given you the choice between life and death, between blessings and curses. Now I call on heaven and earth to witness the choice you make. Oh, that you would choose life, so that you and your descendants might live!

—DEUTERONOMY 30:19

PERSONAL REFLECTION

Are you ready to seek to understand God's plan and purpose for your life and for all life?

PRAYER

Lord, I thank You for my life and for the life of all my brothers and sisters of this human race—born and unborn. Please, Lord, help me be an instrument of peace and healing in this life. I come now asking that Your mercy temper the judgment we surely deserve.

Teach us, Your people, to pray in deep and sincere repentance, asking for Your forgiveness of our sins. Where we should be living together as one race, we as a nation have rejected Your truth in Acts 17:26 of one blood/one human race and embraced ethnic division leading to the injustice of racism. We have slaughtered our weakest: the babies in the womb, the poor, the elderly, and the infirm in the name of reproductive rights and social justice. We have embraced inhumanity to humankind in the name of humanism.

In constructing and destroying man-made statues in the name of memorials, we have worshipped idols and are reaping the bitter grapes of wrath today. O Lord, forgive us. Fan the flames of revival. Today we pray for our leaders, that they will walk in Your ways, accepting the wisdom and godly counsel of Your Word. Breathe, dear Lord, on the White House, the state House, the schoolhouse, the bank house, the sick house, the poorhouse, the jailhouse, the drug house, the whorehouse, the orphan house, the widow's house, the church house, the world house, and my house. O Lord, touch every house and every heart. Give sight to the blind, and set the captives free.

O God, let our nation be reborn in a day. Sanctify our wombs, and let us obey Your Word and rejoice. Bless us, O God. Please bless our leaders, according to

Your Word in 1 Timothy 2:2, that we may live blessed and productive lives. Please let Your justice roll down as waters and Your righteousness as a mighty stream. Help us love You, one another, and ourselves. In Jesus's name, amen.

Here I am at the annual Issues4Life march, along with (from left) Father Frank Pavone, Rev. Clennard Childress, Rev. Walter Hoye, and Janet Morana.

As I advocate for the unborn, I also share my testimony and remind people of God's power to heal and forgive after abortion.

Chapter 16

DIVINE JUSTICE

I hate all your show and pretense—the hypocrisy of your religious festivals and solemn assemblies.... Away with your noisy hymns of praise! I will not listen to the music of your harps. Instead, I want to see a mighty flood of justice, an endless river of righteous living.

—AMOS 5:21, 23–24

WHILE I WAS writing this chapter, a friend made a profound statement as we were having a very precious phone conversation: "God's justice is always righteous and loving." I have reflected on this truth many times over the years, but it seemed appropriate to begin this chapter with this concept. God is love; therefore God's justice and judgments are meted out from His love.

Many people talk about God's love, but His judgment often doesn't get as much attention. Too many Christians hide behind facades, causing their public lives to be inconsistent with their private realities. When I was born again and decided to truly follow and serve God, I became very transparent about my mistakes—alcoholism, fornication, and abortion. Before being born again, I thought those things were OK. When I learned they were not OK, I repented of those mistakes and received God's forgiveness.

That is why I am able to speak about my past without feeling shame or condemnation—it's because of the liberty and the joy I received from God when He forgave me. This is His justice and judgment for all who will come to Him in repentance. We do not have to be fearful and hide from our sins. Jesus paid the price for our sins, and justice was served when He hung on the cross and died in our place. Now we need only repent and receive His forgiveness.

Of course there is more to judgment. There's God's judgment, but there's also our judgment of ourselves. I'm not talking about self-condemnation. Responsible and Holy Spirit–led Christians will be able to look at themselves and ask God to show them anything in their lives that is not aligned with His will for them. Like Job, we can say, "Teach me, and I will keep quiet. Show me what I have done wrong" (Job 6:24). And like David, we can pray,

"Search me, O God, and know my heart; test me and know my anxious thoughts. Point out anything in me that offends you, and lead me along the path of everlasting life" (Ps. 139:23–24). We must be able to humbly judge ourselves and seek God's mercy concerning our own shortcomings before we minister to others and show them where they've gone wrong.

In Matthew 7:5 Jesus teaches us to judge ourselves before we judge others. He says, "Hypocrite! First get rid of the log in your own eye; then you will see well enough to deal with the speck in your friend's eye." God wants us to take a sober look at ourselves. We call this conviction.

Some people think Jesus's words to "not judge others" (Matt. 7:1) mean we should never make mention of another person's sin. But Matthew 7:5 clearly says we must judge ourselves first so we "will see well enough to deal with the speck in [our] friend's eye." That speck, whether in our own eye or a friend's, can keep us off the path God has for us. That's why as members of the body of Christ we should lovingly encourage one another to stay on the path of righteousness.

Gentle reminders that sin is a problem are not hypocritical judgment if we are acting in love. But casting the first stone is bad. Pretending to be pious while living sinfully is bad. We must be able to see our own flaws if we are to encourage others to address their shortcomings. Otherwise our condemnation of sin will be hypocritical. That's why Jesus said to the accusers of the woman caught in the act of adultery, "You who are without sin, cast the first stone." (See John 8:7.) He doesn't expect any of us to be perfect, but He does want us to look first at ourselves before calling out others.

> For the time has come for judgment, and it must begin with God's household. And if judgment begins with us, what

terrible fate awaits those who have never obeyed God's Good News?

—1 PETER 4:17

Every time I judge myself, I end up thanking God for His grace and mercy because I always find myself falling short. I have experienced two abortions and have been married three times. Yet because I have repented, like the woman at the well in John 4 and the woman caught in the act of adultery in John 8, I am forgiven.

LOVE AND JUSTICE—PERFECT PARTNERS

Because many people have a hard time reconciling God's love with His justice, I began to explore the link between the goodness of God and the justice of God. As I did, I discovered two comments made by the esteemed theologians Millard Erickson and Paul Enns that I would like to share with you.

In his widely acclaimed book *Christian Theology*, Erickson explains how love and justice work together:

> Justice means that love must always be shown, whether or not a situation of immediate need presents itself in pressing and vivid fashion. Love in the biblical sense, then, is not merely indulging someone near at hand. Rather, it inherently involves justice as well. This means there will be a concern for the ultimate welfare of all humanity, a passion to do what is right, and enforcement of appropriate consequences for wrong action.
>
> Actually, love and justice have worked together in God's dealing with the human race. God's justice requires that there be payment of the penalty for sin. God's love, however, desires humans to be restored to fellowship with him. The offer of Jesus Christ as the atonement for sin means that both the justice and the love of God have been maintained.[1]

Love and justice combine to combat the sin of racism. There can be no true justice for any members of society until all members are regarded as equal. Unless we as humans truly seek the welfare of all humanity, even to the point of preferring to put others before ourselves, we cannot hope to achieve the love and justice Erickson describes.

To further explore this truth, let us regard this passage in *The Moody Handbook of Theology*, where Enns had this to say about God's love and justice:

> When each attribute is understood in light of the other, love and justice are harmonious. They do not compete with each other, but stand side-by-side in complete harmony.[2]

We can see the harmonious nature of love, righteousness, and justice in the civil rights movement of the twentieth century. Uncle ML and my father worked together during those days to build the Beloved Community, where poverty, hunger, and homelessness would not be tolerated and racism and prejudice in any form would be replaced by a spirit of sisterhood and brotherhood.[3] It is clear to me that God, who is love, was the champion and hero who orchestrated and engineered the remarkable strategies implemented by His human emissaries during the battle for racial equality.

During the twentieth century much of what I learned regarding the relationship among righteousness, justice, judgment, and love was through the civil rights movement led by my uncle ML. Now, in the twenty-first century, the message of the sanctity of life has been added to what I call the justice journey.

Allow me to remind you that each chapter in this book introduces a key to help you unleash your spiritual potential. I am just one person sharing this journey with you. The Holy Spirit is our ultimate teacher and guide. Having said this, please allow me to share some experiences I've had in the quest for justice.

SEEKING JUSTICE IN THE MIDST OF DIVISION

Throughout my lifetime I have experienced the tensions of racism. Racism is rooted in sinful delusion, yet it is very real—and it is unrighteous, unloving, and unjust. I have said several times in this book that as Acts 17:26 says, there is one human race, and the notion that there are different races is a fallacy. But as we discuss justice, I find it necessary to discuss race here as well.

There is something called a dichotomous key, which is "a key for the identification of organisms based on a series of choices between alternative characters."[4] *Dichotomous* means "dividing into two parts."[5] While in God's plan the human race has not been divided into more than two "parts" called separate races, there is a dichotomy in the natural mind that allows people to believe there are many races of humans.

As a result, during the 2016 presidential election racial and religious division escalated to a fever pitch, becoming a major point of contention. Diverse voices were shouting, "Black lives matter," "All lives matter," "No justice, no peace," "Unborn lives matter," "Gay lives matter," "Aborted babies don't matter," "Immigrants matter," "Immigrants don't matter," and on and on. Somehow race relations took center stage.

As has been previously stated, my uncle ML and my father were brothers in the civil rights struggle of the twentieth century. They firmly believed God's justice system for human beings was reflected in a Beloved Community, where all human beings—regardless of ethnic, age, skin color, social, or economic differences—should be treated equally. In many ways their views reflected the foundation of the US Constitution as well as the Holy Bible.

We must understand that the idea that there is a "race war" is a result of the sins of division and strife. The solution is repentance for the sin of racism and correcting the flawed mind-set that has ruled the United States for far too long.

Color-blind theory doesn't help.

We don't have the liberty of covering up this sin with platitudes like color blindness. As Monnica T. Williams states in her *Psychology Today* article, racial color blindness seems like a good thing on the surface, but it is not good enough. She writes:

> At its face value, colorblindness seems like a good thing— really taking MLK seriously on his call to judge people on the content of their character rather than the color of their skin. It focuses on commonalities between people, such as their shared humanity.
>
> However, colorblindness alone is not sufficient to heal racial wounds on a national or personal level. It is only a half-measure that in the end operates as a form of racism.[6]

For the record, before we go any further, no human being is literally black or white. Even the palest Caucasian has beige or pearl undertones. Even the most ebony hue has undertones of purple, blue, and magenta. Human beings have a wide range of skin colors, just as almost every other creation under the sun. So where does this color-blind concept really find its deceptive source?

> I was blind but now I see!
>
> —JOHN 9:25, NIV

In the biological sense, if someone is color-blind, he is considered to have a medical impairment that should be treated. Yet here in twenty-first century America, when discussing issues of race, people will often say, "I don't see color; I am color-blind." On the surface this sounds so sweet and kind, doesn't it? Well, in a spiritual sense, those with this condition are not to be applauded; they need spiritual enlightenment. Why? Because racial color blindness is spiritual blindness, which gives cover to the system that fosters white privilege.

The dangers of privilege

According to essayist Tim Wise, "White privilege refers to any advantage, opportunity, benefit, head start, or general protection from negative societal mistreatment, which persons deemed white will typically enjoy, but which others will generally not enjoy."[7]

He goes on to explain:

> These benefits can be material (such as greater opportunity in the labor market, or greater net worth, due to a history in which whites had the ability to accumulate wealth to a greater extent than persons of color), social (such as presumptions of competence, creditworthiness, law-abidingness, intelligence, etc.) or psychological (such as not having to worry about triggering negative stereotypes, rarely having to feel out of place, not having to worry about racial profiling, etc.).
>
> Operationally, white privilege is simply the flipside of discrimination against people of color. The concept is rooted in the common-sense observation that there can be no down without an up, so that if people of color are the targets of discrimination, in housing, employment, the justice system, or elsewhere, then whites, by definition, are being elevated above those persons of color. Whites are receiving a benefit, vis-a-vis those persons of color: more opportunity *because* those persons of color are receiving less. Although I believe all persons are harmed in the long run by racism and racial

inequity—and thus, white privilege comes at an immense social cost—it still exists as a daily reality throughout the social, political and economic structure of the United States.[8]

Importantly, Wise notes that "the fact that white privilege exists and that all whites have access to various aspects of it, does not, however, mean that all whites are wealthy, or that in competitions for jobs and other opportunities, whites will always win. The fact of general advantage doesn't require unanimity of outcomes favoring whites." What it means, however, is that overall it pays to be a member of the dominant group.[9]

WE ARE ONE RACE: HUMAN

The human race is diverse, with people having various skin colors, body types, hair types, and other cultural and ethnic distinctions. God never intended for these God-approved distinctions to divide human communities.

When God says in the Bible not to marry aliens or foreigners, this is not a racial issue. It is a spiritual matter, as the Bible says believers are not to marry and procreate with devil and demon worshippers; we are not to be unequally yoked (2 Cor. 6:14).

For example, Ruth and Naomi were from different nations and ethnic groups (not different races). Yet Ruth accepted Naomi's God (our God) and was blessed to become part of the lineage of King David and the Lord Jesus. In this and many other instances in Scripture the ethnic distinction did not indicate that people were of different races but of a different culture. We are all part of the same race: the human race.

NOT EVERYONE WANTS JUSTICE FOR ALL

In 1958 Rev. Billy Graham and my uncle ML appeared together and prayed at a revival meeting in New York City. They agreed that at the time the most segregated hour in America was eleven o'clock on Sunday mornings, when for the most part American Christians gathered in racially divided congregations to attend church services. Of course there were exceptions, but there always are. In that meeting Rev. Graham and Uncle ML made a bold move to step outside the boundaries of the traditional church to set an example of how Christians can come together in worship.

Interestingly enough, a deranged woman stabbed Uncle ML in the chest with a letter opener during that visit. She didn't understand or agree with his message of one race, one Beloved Community. She thought he was committing a crime against humanity by considering it acceptable to call Rev. Graham his equal, his brother. The same can be said for those who were reluctant to put Rev. Graham on equal footing with Uncle ML.

It was the love of God in the heart of Uncle ML during those days that rescued him from the operating table to live to write the 1963 "Letter From a Birmingham Jail," which brought the inequity of the American church pews to an even larger audience. Again, Uncle ML was praying and fighting for the walls of injustice to come down and be replaced with the covering and protection of the grace of God for all Americans and all people. This was the Beloved Community my uncle ML and my father longed to see. Indeed, there are many people in the United States and around the world who are still working toward that end.

DIVINE JUSTICE VS. SOCIAL JUSTICE

Before we end our discussion on this important divine key, I want to be clear that the popular concepts *social justice* and *human rights* are not Bible-based principles. While they can be beneficial if applied with genuine compassion toward humanity, they are not to be confused with the divine justice as discussed in this chapter.

Social justice seeks to create a more socially just world. But this type of justice typically is focused on economic egalitarianism rather than heavenly kingdom principles. There is a distinctive difference between egalitarian justice and equality, and the deeper expressions of God's love for all humanity. Equality from a human perspective tends to deal more with material provisions, whereas in the kingdom of God agape love is the equalizer. While human laws can provide limited sources of justice and equality, God's provisions are more complete.

KING FAMILY TRUTH

"It may be true that you can't legislate integration, but you can legislate desegregation. It may be true that morality cannot be legislated, but behavior can be regulated. It may be true that the law cannot change the heart, but it can restrain the heartless. It may be true that the law can't make a man love me, but it can restrain him from lynching me, and I think that's pretty important also. So while the law may not change the hearts of men, it does change the habits of men. And when you change the habits of men, pretty soon the attitudes and the hearts will be changed. And so there is a need for strong legislation constantly to grapple with the problems we face."[10]

—Martin Luther King Jr.

Yes, God's laws are higher than human laws. In His infinite wisdom God knows that as human beings we have certain physiological needs, and His plan for humanity is higher than the provisos of social justice.

SCRIPTURE REFLECTION

When [God's] justice is done, it brings joy to the righteous but terror to evildoers.

—PROVERBS 21:15, NIV

But let justice roll down like waters and righteousness like an ever-flowing stream.

—AMOS 5:24, NASB

PERSONAL REFLECTION

How can you embrace God's plan for justice in your life and ministry?

PRAYER

Heavenly Father, teach me to seek Your justice rather than revenge. I pray in Jesus's name. Amen.

To hear Alveda King's song "Let Freedom Ring," scan the QR code or visit https://tinyurl.com/LetFreedomRingSong.

In 1958 Billy Graham and my uncle ML appeared together
and prayed at a revival meeting in New York City.

In 2017 there was a sense of breakthrough after the painful division that marked the
2016 presidential election. I was there in the Rose Garden on May 4 when President
Donald Trump signed an executive order giving religious groups more freedom
to engage in political speech. After all the controversy and discord, a president
was elected who supports people of faith having a voice in the public square.

Chapter 17

DIVINE FAMILY

The wicked die and disappear, but the family of the godly stands firm.

—PROVERBS 12:7

IN 2016, IN a message to The Elijah List, my good friend pastor Denny Cline wrote that the Lord had revealed to him that "the key to revival is the restoration of family."[1] Just look around, and you'll notice that there has been a serious breakdown of the nurturing, God-centered unit into which human beings are born or adopted and in which they are sustained and loved and matured and taught how to be productive members of society.

With God clearly saying that if we want to see revival in the last days, we must restore the family, I feel it is my duty to share the values and principles that led to my family's sharing the message of God's love for all people. One of the ways I've done this is through books such as this one. All the keys you have read and will read are a result of the faith-filled foundation my family built. God set us in families so we would be protected, loved, and taught about Him.

As you have already come to know, my uncle ML became known as a "prophet of God's love." Because of his legacy I understood early on the message of John 3:16—that God loves us so much that He sacrificed His beloved Son so we could spend eternity with Him. My mother, Naomi Ruth Barber King, often says: "Hate has to be taught. We were created by God to love and be loved." This truth was instilled in me from a very young age and has shaped every member of my family, through every generation.

KING FAMILY TRUTH

"Hate has to be taught. We were created by God to love and be loved."

—Naomi Ruth Barber King

I grew up in a very loving family. For the first twelve years of my life we lived in the King family Birth Home on Auburn

Avenue in Atlanta. Today the home is a historical site, and millions have visited it over the years. I have very fond memories of our lives in that home. There we, and the generations before us, learned about life, God, dreams, and purpose.

We were encouraged to pursue our dreams. We were taught that we could be whatever we set out to be if we had faith and God in our lives. There were few limits to the encouragement to become what we were born to be. Even the cloud of segregation that surrounded us was not heavy enough to destroy our destinies.

My daddy was my hero. Daddy taught me many things, such as how to be a lady; how to swim; how to believe Jesus was the miracle worker the Bible proclaims Him to be; and the importance of family, love, and forgiveness. Daddy gave me a sweet-sixteen party, as he and his parents had done for Mother when she and Daddy were courting. I always felt very blessed to have had such an exceptional father and to have been born into such a loving, talented family.

A GIFTED FAMILY FOR A PURPOSE

Music was a big part of our family life, and I was very likely born "with a song in my heart." Mother often remarks that even as a little girl, I would say to her, "Mommy, I want to sing." She would always say, "Sing, baby."

Of course, I had no idea all those years ago that one day I would become a "musical worshipper." I just knew I had a voice and that I wanted to sing.

My mother had a lovely speaking and singing voice back when I was a child. As it turns out, she was also a musical worshipper. Again, I didn't know that some people with beautiful voices were called to be worshippers of God and not merely performers or entertainers. Mother was and is both a singer and a worshipper. One day I would become one too.

During the civil rights movement my mother, paternal grandmother, and aunts Christine King Farris and Coretta Scott King often used their gifts of singing and playing instruments to advance the kingdom of God. They also used their musical gifts to sing at fundraising concerts for the Kentucky Christian Leadership Conference and the Southern Christian Leadership Conference, founded by my father and my uncle ML, respectively.

The three preachers' wives—my grandmother, "Big Mama"; Aunt Coretta; and my mother, Naomi King—were the "first ladies" of their husbands' churches. Big Mama was the director of music at Ebenezer Baptist Church in Atlanta, where her husband, known as "Daddy King," was the senior pastor. She played the organ and piano, and there were several choirs.

Many members of my family were Christian civil rights leaders. Others of us were educators, poets, musicians, and singers. While we each were uniquely gifted by God for a specific purpose, our family had a strong unified purpose that gave us focus and motivation to accomplish the things we have become known for.

One of my family's favorite passages of Scripture is found in the Book of Psalms:

> If the LORD does not build the house, it is useless for the builders to work on it. If the LORD does not protect a city, it is useless for the guard to stay alert. It is useless to work hard for the food you eat by getting up early and going to bed late. The LORD gives food to those he loves while they sleep. Children are an inheritance from the LORD. They are a reward from him. The children born to a man when he is young are like arrows in the hand of a warrior. Blessed is the man who has filled his quiver with them. He will not

be put to shame when he speaks with his enemies in the city gate.

—Psalm 127:1–5, gw

Each generation of my family has been taught to honor and worship God with our whole lives, and we revisit that truth with our children and grandchildren every chance we get. Even the older ones such as myself need a refresher course from time to time. This knowledge from Psalm 127 has shaped and guided us, and it has helped us become the people God called us to be.

I know not everyone grows up in a loving family and has godly principles instilled in him from a young age. Some children are raised in two-parent homes, some become orphans, some are adopted, and some experience the brokenness of divorce or the challenges of being raised by single parents or in nontraditional settings. If there is brokenness and hurt from family relationships, choose to forgive and seek healing, which we will discuss in chapter 19, "Divine Relationships." If you're not sure of who you are, or if you know you don't want to be like the people who raised you, ask God to reveal to you who you are in Him and help you create a new and better legacy than the one you inherited.

No matter what the situation with our natural families happens to be, we have a heavenly Father who created us and loves us and wants us to be part of His family. He knew us before we were born and has a good plan for our lives (Jer. 29:11). We have the opportunity to become His children and to spend our lives becoming more like Him. There is eternal hope in this truth.

Scripture Reflection

God sets the lonely in families, he leads out the prisoners with singing.

—Psalm 68:6, niv

...to all who believed him and accepted him, he gave the right to become children of God.

—John 1:12

Personal Reflection

What is the legacy of your family? What are the special gifts and callings unique to your natural bloodline? What are the benefits of being a son or daughter of God?

Prayer

Dear heavenly Father, thank You for my family, such as it is. Help me know that You do not make mistakes. Thank You for making a way for me to be part of Your eternal family. Please help me be a better family member and love and forgive my family even as You love and forgive me. In Jesus's name I pray. Amen.

 To hear Alveda King's song "Bless This House," scan the QR code or visit https://tinyurl.com/BlessThisHouse.

Here is the King family at Thanksgiving in 1963. Pictured from left to right are: (standing) my uncle Martin Luther King Jr. and my aunt Coretta Scott King; my aunt Christine King Farris and my uncle Isaac Farris Sr.; my parents, Naomi and A. D. King; (seated) my brother Alfred King II; my cousins Yolanda King and Martin King III; my brother Vernon King; my grandmother Alberta "Big Mama" King; me holding my cousin Isaac Farris Jr.; my grandfather Martin "Granddaddy" King Sr.; my cousin Dexter King; and my siblings Darlene King and Derek King Sr.

This photo, given to me by my aunt Coretta, shows her, Uncle ML, and Daddy participating in the historic 1965 march from Selma to Montgomery, Alabama.

Chapter 18

DIVINE INTIMACY

For you are my hiding place; you protect me from trouble.
You surround me with songs of victory [deliverance].

—PSALM 32:7

Throughout our journey we have discussed the importance of choosing to obey God and the power of submitting our wills to Him. Now it's time to go a little deeper. Intimacy with God is about deepening our connection with Him and becoming more sensitive to His voice and the movement of His Spirit. God must be the object of our affection. Intimacy with Him transcends any form of human-to-human intimacy. It is through divine intimacy that our spirits and souls are regenerated in Christ and we draw closer to God as our Abba, our Father.

As humans we are not born holy. Although we are created in the image and likeness of God (Gen. 1:27), we are born into sin (Ps. 51:5). This is why Jesus proclaimed that we must be born again (John 3:5), regenerated by accepting the gift of salvation Jesus purchased when He shed His blood on the cross. Then we can be empowered by the infilling of the Holy Spirit, our Comforter and teacher, to carry out His will for our lives. We are sanctified in the regeneration process and are made holy, for the Scriptures say, "You must be holy because I am holy" (1 Pet. 1:16).

As author Oswald Chambers explained, "Redemption [regeneration] means that I can be delivered from the heredity of sin, and that through Jesus Christ I can receive a pure and spotless heredity, namely, the Holy Spirit."[1]

MY FIRST INTIMATE ENCOUNTERS WITH GOD

Through the years, both before and after I was born again, I have had many close encounters with the Lord. In earlier chapters I shared my born-again encounter and brief versions of these testimonies. Here I'd like to revisit two intimate encounters I had with God before I was born again. One saved me from giving up on life when I was away in college in a lonely dorm room. The other literally saved me from being electrocuted by a lightning bolt. Both made me profoundly aware of God's hand on my life.

Don't give up—you have the victory.

My first personal and intimate encounter with God came when I was alone in my bed in my college dorm room. I was at a very low point in my life. I had just returned to my room from a confrontation with my boyfriend. You may recall that I shared some of this story in a previous chapter. We had been in a very volatile argument during which he shook me violently by my shoulders and even put his hands around my throat as he yelled at me to shut up. I was saying some pretty angry words, taking out my frustrations on him. We were both very angry and very wrong because the world was upside down and we didn't have enough of God in our lives to help us handle our situations.

I remember being aware that I was floating up and out of my body. I was floating up through the treetops, and I could see my boyfriend shaking me. I couldn't physically feel anything anymore. It was like I was there and yet not there. I heard him screaming my name: "Alveda! Wake up! Come back!"

While I don't pretend to be like the apostle Paul, caught up in the Spirit of God during that moment, my experience reminded me of what he shares in 2 Corinthians 12:2-4 (NIV):

> I know a man in Christ who fourteen years ago was caught up to the third heaven. Whether it was in the body or out of the body I do not know—God knows. And I know that this man—whether in the body or apart from the body I do not know, but God knows—was caught up to paradise and heard inexpressible things, things that no one is permitted to tell.

Though my experience in the natural was very different from this passage, I will tell you this: I believe God was close at that time, and I didn't want to come back from my out-of-body journey. It was very pleasant. The air was warm and balmy, not hot. The treetops were like feathers around me, and the sky was infinitely beautiful. I was headed away from my problems. Somehow, though, I floated back into my body.

A few days before, I had broken a friendship with my roommate. My uncle ML had been assassinated a few months earlier, and many of my relationships were in flux. I was angry with God, the world, and, sadly, white people. My daddy had begged me to forgive James Earl Ray, the man who had shot Uncle ML, and not to blame white people because there were some really good white people who prayed with us, marched with us, lived with us, and died with us. But I wasn't ready to do that, so I argued with my then roommate and blamed her for the sins of the world. That argument had landed me in the little one-person college dorm room.

I was alone, angry, desolate, and feeling as if I had no one to turn to. I was away from my home, my parents, and my family. I wasn't living a Christian life and had fallen prey to the secular, humanistic curriculum being taught in so many colleges and universities those days. I had even begun to question my faith in God. As I sat in my dorm room all alone in that heartless state, I began to think morbid thoughts. Drowning in my self-pity, I wanted to die.

Suddenly, seemingly out of nowhere, an audible, deep voice—booming, yet quiet—asked a question, "Are you ready to die yet?" Thinking back on it, I realize the voice was asking me if I really wanted death, or if I actually wanted to live. I remember lying there quietly, no longer afraid or troubled. I thought about the question and answered: "I'm not ready to die. I want to have children."

Ever since I was a little girl, I had told my parents that I wanted six children when I grew up. That desire was so strong in my heart that even at my lowest moment, when I felt like giving up, I knew I wanted to be a mother one day. I was still a virgin, and I was troubled, but I understood that motherhood was part of my destiny.

As I look back today, as a mother of six and grandmother of ten (and ready for more!), I realize that I have benefited from the prayers of my ancestors throughout my life. God's grace has covered me, even when I wasn't aware of it. There are generational curses and generational blessings. The prayers of our elders can keep hope alive from generation to generation. I believe it was because of those prayers that I didn't die in that dorm room.

I finished out that semester and returned home to my parents and siblings. Soon we moved from Kentucky back to Atlanta, where Daddy became the co-pastor of Ebenezer Baptist Church with Granddaddy because Uncle ML was dead.

Our world was upside down. My parents and grandparents were still grieving the death of Uncle ML. Daddy was trying to pick up the pieces of the movement his brother had led. Daddy was like Bobby Kennedy without John, the biblical Aaron without Moses, James the disciple without John. He was like a son of thunder alone without his lightning-force brother. Granddaddy and Big Mama were stoic but not the same strong tower they had been for so many years. Mother tried to console Daddy, but he wouldn't let her into his grief. He cried alone every night.

In the midst of all of this, I got married. Some of my girlfriends from Kentucky and my best friend from childhood were my bridesmaids. Daddy marched his virgin baby girl down the wedding aisle. Then, a week later, Daddy was killed and thrown into our swimming pool at home. Just like that he joined Uncle ML in heaven. These sons of thunder were reunited forever. After all this I was a very broken and confused young lady.

Before you mistake this for a pity party, rest assured that God's love and mercy won out even through those dark days. There would be more bumps and tumbles ahead, but God was working on me, and the outcome would be victory.

Lightning doesn't strike twice.

A few years later, when I was in my mid-twenties, I was divorced, rebellious, and in denial of my self-imposed distance from God. I was the mother of a young son at the time, had suffered a miscarriage, and was post-abortive, hiding my secrets from the world. I had taken to drowning my sorrows in bourbon, hanging out in nightclubs, and singing karaoke for applause and approval from lonely people like me. Still I somehow managed to tell myself that I was on top of the world.

One particular night, I was at a club with a friend. We would often go out for drinks and then drive home alone. As I mentioned in a previous chapter, that evening, I had one more drink than I typically allowed myself, and I became tipsy. It was just about time to go home, and I headed toward the car. My friend begged me not to drive home. She and others in our crowd were truly concerned. But I remember saying something flippant and cavalier to them like, "Oh, don't worry. My car is like an old horse. She knows her way home." And somehow I bobbed and weaved myself toward home.

About five blocks from the house, the bottom fell out of the sky. Torrential rain pummeled the streets, trees, and my car. Lightning hit a tree in front of me, and it crashed to the ground. When it fell, a live electric wire broke loose from the power box and landed across the hood of my car. I was tipsy, but I hit the brakes and brought the car to a hard stop.

Before I could reach for the key in the ignition and grab the door handle to exit the vehicle, both being natural responses to the crisis upon me, I heard an audible voice say, "Be still and know that I am God!" I became instantly sober. I was in awe of the voice, the rain, and the dark sky. A deep and sudden peace came over me. I knew God had come and invaded my storm. I'm not sure if I stayed in that moment for a few minutes or several hours, but I will never forget how I felt.

An emergency response team came down the street and removed the wire from the car. Sparks were still popping from the wire as they worked. A man looked inside and tapped on the window. He said, "Miss, are you OK?" I nodded, "Yes, I am," and opened the door.

He said: "We were wondering. That was a live wire. If you had touched your keys or the door handle, you would have been fried."

Years later, after I became born-again, I often reflected on those early miracles where God kept me alive. I began to experience increasing evidence of God's grace in my life. Even after my second divorce God was there. I truly have experienced wonderful times alone with God.

GOD'S PRESENCE BRINGS HEALING

Sometime after my young children and I were able to move into a brand-new model home in a lovely little subdivision, I had developed a daily custom of Bible reading and listening for God's voice in the midst of life's chatter. On one particular day, I sensed God calling me to come and spend time with Him, but I wanted to do other things. I bustled around cleaning the house, making phone calls, cooking, washing clothes, and just filling each moment, drowning out God's voice.

Finally it was time for me to take a shower. The bathroom was very pretty. It even had an oval garden tub. The house was quiet because the children were away with family. As I got things ready, the running water quieted my busy mind.

Suddenly the bathroom filled with the presence of God! It was a tangible presence, so real, so consuming, and so very intimate.

I jumped out of the shower, and I ran from the bathroom, almost yelling, "OK, God!"

This was the beginning of an increasing awareness of God's desire to bring me closer into His presence. A few years later, when I joined the pro-life ministry of Priests for Life, I had the blessing of talking with Theresa Burke, PhD, cofounder of the post-abortion healing ministry Rachel's Vineyard. Because Theresa is very intuitive, she led me into a conversation about post-abortion healing. As I was sitting on the couch before her, Theresa asked me about my relationship with God. She told me I should learn to forgive myself, release God from blame, and allow Him to heal me from all my past hurts.

I remember sliding to the end of the couch and curling my arms around my body. Theresa asked me if I realized what I had just done. I told her yes, I understood that in sliding to the end of the couch, I was attempting to move away from Theresa and God. From that moment until now I began to run closer to God. I stopped running away.

A few weeks after that conversation with Theresa I was ready to participate in the healing ministry of Rachel's Vineyard. At the beginning of the weekend all participants, both men and women, were directed to a pile of rocks and stones of different colors and sizes. We were invited to take a rock and carry it as a representation of our burdens and to return the selected stone to the pile when we felt ready to release it.

During that weekend retreat we completed scriptural healing exercises and reenacted scenes from biblical figures such as the woman at the well and the woman with the issue of blood. At one point a priest stood in, representing Jesus, and asked: "What would you have the Lord do for you today?" In response we cast our cares upon the waters by placing lighted floating candles in a large basin of water.

All the exercises of faith and healing at Rachel's Vineyard retreats are inspired by Bible testimonies. The hours I spent there brought me much healing and comfort. As a result of this deeper level of healing, I've been able to serve as a national spokesperson for post-abortion healing, as well as work with Silent No More Awareness cofounders Janet Morana and Georgette Forney to promote a vital education campaign focusing on the harmful impact of abortion. I believe that my becoming closer to God enables me to have the strength to do this work.

KING FAMILY TRUTH

"The end of life is not to be happy, nor to achieve pleasure and avoid pain, but to do the will of God, come what may."[2]

—Martin Luther King Jr.

ONLY ONE THING TRULY SATISFIES

A few years ago someone asked me, "What is the one thing that would really satisfy you, complete you? Is it a really big best-selling book? Is it producing and acting in a blockbuster movie or making a fortune? What do you really want out of life?"

Mind you, I was almost sixty-five years old at the time. I had been blessed to accomplish many things in my life, and if I had a bucket list, I couldn't readily rattle off what items I'd put on it.

As I contemplated this person's question, I thought back to the days when I wanted some of the things this person had named. I knew I couldn't take this question lightly because this person had the ability to open many doors and possibly could have helped to make happen anything I wanted.

However, in all honesty, I couldn't imagine any earthly thing that could fill the "God hole" in my soul. Oh, I am still human enough to appreciate the creature comforts of life, and God is so good to me that I have my share of blessings in this life. Yet these blessings don't complete me.

It is in this place of intimacy with God that I always hope to remain. After experiencing the ups and downs of life, I want to always come back to the realization that only Jesus can truly satisfy my soul desires. I've written about how important praise and worship are for me. There are songs such as "Jesus, You're the Center of My Joy," "I Give Myself Away," and the hymn "I Surrender All" that correspond with Bible passages from King David's intimate conversations with God. Spending time in deep worship can be an invaluable way to build an ongoing intimate relationship with God.

You may be saying, "Alveda, I'm not a singer," or you may lament, "I'm not a poet like King David." Well, God isn't looking for singers and poets, although those are beautiful gifts. What God desires is obedient hearts that genuinely long to worship Him—and not just in public but also in private. God loves to have intimate communion with us.

We should welcome what Oswald Chambers referred to as the haunting presence of God: "If we are haunted by God, nothing else can get in, no cares, no tribulation, no anxieties. We see now why Our Lord so emphasized the sin of worry. How can we dare be so utterly unbelieving when God is round about us."[3]

God's presence is everything to a person who wants to walk fully free, victorious, and unbound. His presence gives us the power to live in the full expression of His perfect will for our lives. Blogger John Barry wrote that "when we align ourselves with who God created us to be, our desires become His desires. Our thirst for gain is quenched by God...We...understand our role in God's work and request [of God] what we need to fulfill that role, trusting that He will provide the rest."[4] And we discover that our cup overflows.

The Bible says that God will give us the desires of our hearts. What else could be more satisfying?

UNBLOCK THE SPIRITUAL ARTERIES OF YOUR HEART

Consider how so many people are being advised to take medicine to unblock their arteries and correct the blood flow to their hearts. Somehow how a heart that is spiritually clogged needs to be unblocked is much like the biological heart that is damaged by blocked arteries. We know that bad food and bad habits can cause biological heart blockage. What causes spiritual heart blockage?

Hatred, strife, fear, anxiety, and a host of harmful emotional baggage can cause our hearts to falter. That's why the Bible warns us to guard our hearts. (See Proverbs 4:23.) We need to unblock the arteries of our spiritual hearts with the love, power, and presence of God. As we unblock our hearts, we increase the flow of the blood of Jesus. As we unblock our spiritual hearts, we can experience healing in our natural bodies as well as in the body of Christ.

The anointing of God is revealed, expressed, and released in the presence of God. The *rhema* word (revealed knowledge of God) comes to us in these precious, intimate moments. Sometimes we may feel we need a special closet or secret place to meet God, but our ultimate secret place with God is in our hearts.

Psalm 91:1 says, "He who dwells in the secret place of the Most High shall abide under the shadow of the Almighty" (NKJV). As humans we live in our homes. We take vacations to special places. We follow our daily routines, going to work and attending to the affairs of life. So how can we *dwell* with God if we can only meet

Him at assigned physical locations? We must make permanent room for God in the secret place of our hearts. Fill that room, that "God hole," with the presence of God, the Holy Spirit.

Along with having this permanent room for God, much like the Shunammite woman in 2 Kings 4 who reserved a special chamber in her home for the man of God, we can also have special locations in our earthly abodes where we enjoy the presence of God.

Throughout the years, wherever I roam and settle, I consecrate space in what I call my "secret garden." When my children were young, we would sit in the garden and talk to God together. We still do. My little grandchildren have enjoyed many secret-garden experiences with me as well. I also have secret prayer spaces in my homes and vacation spots. My family and I enjoy moments when we can "steal away to Jesus" in those secret places.

I encourage you to seek and enjoy your own intimate and secret places, where you and you alone can meet God and experience His divine intimacy. He holds the keys and extends them to you.

SCRIPTURE REFLECTION

For as the earth brings forth its sprouts, and as a garden causes what is sown in it to sprout up, so the Lord GOD will cause righteousness and praise to sprout up before all the nations.

—ISAIAH 61:11, ESV

Come close to God, and God will come close to you. Wash your hands, you sinners; purify your hearts, for your loyalty is divided between God and the world.

—JAMES 4:8

PERSONAL REFLECTION

Search your heart. Have you been avoiding close encounters with God by filling your days with busy tasks? Take time to write down how you can find more time alone with God.

PRAYER

Dear heavenly Father, help me clear my calendar, my desk, my life, or at least be able to turn away from all of that for a while to spend time with You. This I pray in Jesus's name. Amen.

Chapter 19

DIVINE SEXUALITY

Then God blessed them and said, "Be fruitful and multiply. Fill
the earth and govern it. Reign over the fish in the sea, the birds
in the sky, and all the animals that scurry along the ground."

—GENESIS 1:28

Because of Satan's hatred for God he has waged an all-out war on God's creation. One of the ways he has done this is through sexuality—God's procreative plan for the human race to thrive, multiply, and subdue the earth. His evil tactics in this area often show themselves through child molestation, human sex trafficking, homosexuality, porn addiction, adultery, fornication, abortion, rape, divorce, and so many other misuses of human sexuality.

As a result of the confusion these evil tactics have caused, humanity has debated what expressions of human sexuality are appropriate for as long as we have been around. Searching for the answers, people have indulged in sexual activity inside and outside the structure God ordained for the procreation and longevity of the human family. We've asked ourselves, Is sex wrong? Is sex dirty? Is sex right? Is sex good?

The answers lie in the perspectives of those asking the questions. Even the definition of *sex* is often unclear these days. For instance, someone might ask, "What sex are you?" But we are left to wonder whether the person is asking what gender we are. If gender is what the person is seeking to know, it would be better to ask, "What is your gender?" But then this question often causes its own brand of confusion because in the ongoing quest for enlightenment some people are confused about their gender.

A person could be born as anatomically male yet "feel" more female than male. The same can be said of some women who "feel" more male than female. This is not an all-encompassing picture of the way the devil has come after our sexuality, but this shows us where we find ourselves as we attempt to find our way back to God's original plan for us.

In my early years I experienced my own times of sexual confusion. As a cherished and beloved child in what would become the famous King family, I should have been protected from sexual predators. Without the knowledge of my parents and grand parents I fell victim to a teenage neighbor when I was ten. He was seventeen and touched me inappropriately when he walked me to the store and back. Afterward he gave me candy and warned me not to tell "our secret." This was very confusing to me because I wasn't sure why I couldn't tell.

Two years later I was still pretty confused about sexuality, but I wasn't sure whom to talk to about it or what to say. I eventually talked to another neighbor, an older girl who was my babysitter. I told her what the boy had done, and she asked me to show her. The sad thing is she ended up touching me too, leading to more confusion.

Today we would call this child molestation. My innocence had been sorely violated, and I was ashamed. I kept those experiences a secret even after I got married. Although I was a "virgin" bride, I was far from innocent because of the previous violations.

Later the sin of abortion was added to my list of guilty secrets, and I became more private about my sexuality, adding secrets to secrets and pain on top of pain. In my twenties, after my divorce, I was a victim of date rape. It was painful and terrible, yet it was another secret I added to my growing list.

Yes, I kept these incidents secret until many years later, when young victims of similar and worse incidents came to share their stories with me. Needless to say, I remembered my pain and was very careful not to continue this destructive pattern. I respected and valued the little ones who were seeking my help. I thank God that He broke the cycle.

Freedom, forgiveness, healing, and restoration came as I shared my testimony. I shared it all—the molestation and abortion accounts, the adultery and fornication, the rape, and finally the redemption trail that led to my being born again and healed.

I was able to assure the ones who came to me that their victimization was not their fault, and I helped them to forgive those who hurt them. I encouraged them to seek forgiveness, restoration, redemption, and inner healing for themselves, as I had done.

SIN DESTROYED GOD'S PERFECT DESIGN

As we know, women are not the only ones to suffer such attacks from the enemy. Though they don't report the incidents as often as women do, many gay men also have stories of early childhood sexual violations that left them broken and ashamed. Their pain is often compounded when they have parents who hit and condemn them when they acknowledge they have homosexual desires. I believe parents whose children tell them they are attracted to the same sex should respond with truth, love, and compassion, not angry attacks.[1]

Some people believe it is God's design that certain individuals are gay or lesbian. I wonder, then, if they also believe it is God's will that people have diabetes or high blood pressure. Do they feel it is God's will that some are poor and hungry? Otherwise why else would they reason, "If God had wanted a person to be straight, He would have made him that way. Since God is God, couldn't He change these things if they are not His will?"

Because someone is born with a particular bent, the assumption has been that God created him that way. The good news is that God designs each of us to be whole and perfect. No matter how we are born and what degree of sin and iniquity is part of our birth (including sickness and disease caused by the fallen state of our world), the really good news is that we can be born again!

The bad news is that sin entered the world when Adam and Eve disobeyed God's command, disturbing the perfect design of humanity and short-circuiting the perfect plan of creation. Since then sin has been transmitted from generation to generation through DNA and RNA. God desires for all members of the human race to be whole, healthy, and blessed in every way. Evil forces are the originators of sickness, disease, and poverty. God, on the other hand, is love, and He is good!

Distrust in God's Word leads to sin and confusion.

For Christians, the Bible helps us understand the origins of sin, sickness, disease, poverty, and all other harmful influences that affect the procreative human family. However, some people do not trust the Bible. "The Bible was written by the white man," they say. "You can't trust *their* Bible because they used it to enslave us." While it is true that some slave masters twisted the truths of the Bible for their own dark purposes, it doesn't mean the Bible itself is twisted. The humans who did evil things were twisted.

Have you ever heard anyone say, "The white man used money to enslave us, so we can't use money," or "The white man made us pick cotton, so we can't wear cotton"? Of course not.

Distrust in the inerrancy of God's Word is not only something black Americans wrestle with; people of various ethnic identities have trouble believing the truth of the Bible or have misinterpreted its recounting of the goodness of God. Some even try to use the Bible to justify certain lifestyle choices involving sexuality, money, and so on. People twist the Bible to accommodate their personal desires all the time, no matter what color they are. But the fact remains that the Bible is true and can always be trusted.

Distrust in God's Word leads to generational curses.

The spoken word of God can be traced back to the creation of the world and all the life in it. (See Genesis 1.) The origin of sin and iniquity goes back almost as far. (See Genesis 3.) They are ancient partners with sickness and disease. But God has a prescription for living good and happy lives.

> If you will listen carefully to the voice of the LORD your God and do what is right in his sight, obeying his commands and keeping all his decrees, then I will not make you suffer any of the diseases I sent on the Egyptians; for I am the LORD who heals you.
>
> —EXODUS 15:26

The results of humanity's choice to disobey God—sin and iniquity and sickness and disease of the body, mind, and spirit—have been imprinted on our DNA and RNA, showing up in our family lines one generation after another. The recurring battle with sin and sickness is related to what are called generational curses. Think about it: Mama was diabetic, and so is the child. Papa had high blood pressure, and so does the child. The Bible says in Numbers 14:18:

> The LORD is slow to anger and filled with unfailing love, forgiving every kind of sin and rebellion. But he does not excuse the guilty. He lays the sins of the parents upon their children; the entire family is affected—even children in the third and fourth generations.

Sickness and sin entered the human family with the fall of man, but there is a divine cure—and that cure is Jesus! If someone has cancer, diabetes, or hypertension, he or she will run to the doctor. Sickness feels bad, so we try to get rid of it. Sin ultimately feels bad too, but even though we have a great Physician in Jesus Christ, we are not so quick to look for deliverance or healing from sin. It just seems easier in our sinful minds to try to find a way and a reason to keep sinning because for the moment it feels good. And as a result, we go deeper and deeper into sin. Yet there is an answer to our problems. We just have to turn away from sin and turn to God.

Distrust in God's Word leads us to harmful desires.

> Don't you realize that those who do wrong will not inherit the Kingdom of God? Don't fool yourselves. Those who indulge in sexual sin, or who worship idols, or commit adultery, or are male prostitutes, or practice homosexuality, or are thieves, or greedy people [gluttons], or drunkards, or are abusive, or cheat people—none of these will inherit the Kingdom of God.
>
> —1 CORINTHIANS 6:9–10

When the Word of God is not our foundation for living, we crave drugs, harmful foods, money, sex, and the like. The Bible calls this lust of the flesh. Some people try to get rid of lust and various addictions, such as compulsive gambling, gluttony, and drugs, through twelve-step programs. But they resort to such measures only when they are at risk of losing everything—when instead of the good feelings they've been chasing, they are faced with the rock-bottom reality of their choices.

Distrust in God's Word leads to wrong thinking.

In our postmodern society the things that were once wrong are being challenged as natural and needing our tolerance and acceptance. When our flesh burns for sexual release from someone else's spouse or someone underage or a same-sex partner, there are those who would fight to legitimize and protect these expressions of human sexuality.

For example, why is homosexuality a protected category? Perhaps for the same reason there is one category of protected murder in our country (abortion). This is not right thinking, according to God's Word. Abortion kills babies, yet abortion is legal. It's as if our society is so worried about hurting people's feelings that we fight to uphold same-sex lifestyles and kill babies.

Though some have challenged the position my uncle ML took on these issues, *Ebony* magazine published an advice column he wrote in the 1950s that revealed his thinking on these issues:

> **Question:** My problem is different from the ones most people have. I am a boy, but I feel about boys the way I ought to feel about girls. I don't want my parents to know about me. What can I do?

> **Answer:** Your problem is not at all an uncommon one. However, it does require careful attention. The type of feeling that you have toward boys is probably not an innate tendency, but something that has been culturally acquired....You are already on the right road toward a solution, since you honestly recognize the problem and have a desire to solve it.[2]

When we believe God's Word, we develop honesty with ourselves about what God says is His design for humanity. Here is what Uncle ML said in response to a reader's guilt over an abortion his girlfriend had.

> **Question:** About two years ago, I was going with a young lady who became pregnant. I refused to marry her. As a result, I was directly responsible for a crime. It was not until a month later that I realized the awful thing I had done. I begged her to forgive me, to come back, but she has not answered my letters. The thing stays on my mind. What can I do? I have prayed for forgiveness.

> **Answer:** You have made a mistake....One can never rectify a mistake until he admits that a mistake has been made. Now that you have prayed for forgiveness and acknowledged your mistake, you must turn your vision to the future....Now that you have repented, don't concentrate on

what you failed to do in the past, but what you are deter-mined to do in the future.[3]

Consider this: homosexuality and abortion share a common denominator—they both attack the foundations of procreation and the human family. The sex act between two men or two women cannot result in conception of another human being. Abortion cuts off the life of the person in the womb.

When we twist the Bible to fit our lifestyle rather than twisting our lives to meet God's ideals, we end up lost and confused. God's Word is a light to our paths and a lamp to our feet (Ps. 119:105). It illuminates our paths to live out His will for us. God's Word is not about hard rules and regulations; it is actually an expression of His love for us.

In order to believe this truth, we must seek to receive a renewed mind. When we ask, the Holy Spirit reveals to us the right way to read God's Word and apply its principles to our lives. Through divine revelation and understanding we will come to know the Bible as the divine manual for living on this earth. Without it—especially the commandment to love God, ourselves, and our neighbors—we are a lost and lawless people.

"Born That Way"

Psalm 51:5 says, "For I was born a sinner—yes, from the moment my mother conceived me." And in Romans 3:23 we find that "everyone has sinned; we all fall short of God's glorious standard." With everyone being "born a sinner," people can be born with all types of issues and conditions, including sexual issues. We have already discussed that there are hereditary diseases and genera-tional curses that pass from one generation to the next. Some have debated whether same-sex desire is a sin issue that a person could be born with. I believe that is possible.

I believe Jesus shed some light on this issue in Matthew 19:8–12:

> Jesus replied, "Moses permitted divorce only as a concession to your hard hearts, but it was not what God had originally intended. And I tell you this, whoever divorces his wife and marries someone else commits adultery—unless his wife has been unfaithful."
>
> Jesus' disciples then said to him, "If this is the case, it is better not to marry!"
>
> "Not everyone can accept this statement," Jesus said. "Only those whom God helps. Some are born as eunuchs, some have been made eunuchs by others, and some choose not to marry for the sake of the Kingdom of Heaven. Let anyone accept this who can."

In Scripture a eunuch was a male who would not or could not have sex with a woman. There are at least three groups of people who were defined as eunuchs in biblical times, which can be seen in the passage in Matthew 19:[4]

1. The eunuch who would not have sex for religious purposes (and perhaps entered a monastery).

2. The eunuch who was castrated (typically to work in harems).

3. The eunuch who from birth was physically unable to engage in sexual activity or, possibly, was born with no sexual interest in women.

Even this does not mean these men were created that way. Remember, Jesus said, "Some are born as eunuchs." The problem is some people think Jesus was condoning same-sex desire by saying this, but He wasn't. He was simply explaining why some men could refrain from sexual activity and marriage. The whole chapter of Matthew 19 deals with human sexuality and affirms sex within the bounds of marriage between one man and one woman.

It is important to understand that homosexuality wasn't part of God's original design. The meddling usurper—the devil—stole the keys to the laboratory and disturbed perfection. He tried to make an unnatural thing natural. This was not God's doing. Because of sin we are born with unnatural inclinations that feel natural. That is the deception of Satan. What may feel natural because of the fall of Adam and Eve in the Garden of Eden is not necessarily what is holy. First Peter 1:15 says, "Be holy in everything you do, just as God who chose you is holy."

God has made absolutely no modifications to His original plan for the male and female models He created at the beginning of time. He has not changed His purpose for us to "be fruitful and multiply" and to "fill the earth and govern it" (Gen. 1:28).

A HOLY UNION

The Christian church has the best-kept secret around—married sex is the best sex! Any sex outside of God-ordained marriage is counterfeit, is often unfulfilling, and leads to any number of open doors for soul ties and other spiritual enemies to creep into your life. This includes adultery, homosexuality, pornography, sex trafficking, fornication, sexually transmitted diseases, low self-esteem, heartbreak, bitterness, rejection, and so on.

We need to realize that sex between one man and one woman who love each other and submit to each other in marriage is liberating. In such instances neither the redeemed husband nor his redeemed wife is under the curse of Adam and Eve. The man is not trying to rule over his wife, as he was cursed to do because of Adam's and Eve's sins. (See Genesis 3:16–17.) Instead, the redeemed husband loves his wife as Christ loved the church and sacrificed Himself for it. The wife's desire is not unnaturally directed toward her husband, as in the curse of Eve, but she is at liberty to express her godly desires and free to love and respect her husband as unto the Lord. (See Ephesians 5:21–33.) Together they can enjoy their mutual sexuality in the bonds of holy matrimony, as God always intended.

The most romantic love stories in the Bible are between married people. Sensual love is approved within marriage, as we see in the following passages from the Song of Solomon.

"O rarest of beautiful women, where has your loved one gone? We will help you find him."

The Girl: "He has gone down to his garden, to his spice beds, to pasture his flock and to gather the lilies. I am my beloved's and my beloved is mine...."

King Solomon: "O my beloved, you are as beautiful as the lovely land of Tirzah, yes, beautiful as Jerusalem, and how you capture my heart. Look the other way, for your eyes have overcome me! Your hair, as it falls across your face, is like a flock of goats frisking down the slopes of Gilead."

—Song of Solomon 6:1–5, TLB

Come, my beloved, let us go to the countryside, let us spend the night in the villages. Let us go early to the vineyards to see if the vines have budded, if their blossoms have opened, and if the pomegranates are in bloom—there I will give you my love. The mandrakes send out their fragrance, and at our door is every delicacy, both new and old, that I have stored up for you, my beloved.

—Song of Solomon 7:11–13, NIV

In these passages the king and his bride express godly sexual desire for each other. Sex in marriage is desirable and good. This is something that should be taught to our children so they remember when they become adults. It is so much easier to teach biblical human sexuality from the beginning than to undo the work of the devil once ungodly ideas about sexuality take hold. Don't be afraid to teach your children about sex and marriage. There are great benefits and rewards!

Godly sex is the real thing. "Godly sex?" you may ask. Yes. Who do you think created sex in the first place? Sex is beautiful and God-ordained when it is enjoyed in marriage between one man and one woman. Within biblical marriage it can be enjoyed at its most fulfilling and rewarding level.

RESTORING GOD'S DESIGN

There are obviously destructive forces at work to attack the pro-creative human family, and these forces are not readily and easily perceived by the human senses. Any force that short-circuits a person's life span and/or circumvents someone's procreative energy cannot be good. But God has already won this battle through His Son, who has given us back the authority to quench the fiery darts of the enemy and stand in this evil day. So what does this look like in our everyday lives? I am going to give you five practical ways you can begin to live out with authority the key of divine sexuality. The Bible says to resist the devil, and he will flee from you. Here are ways you can do that:

1. Come to Jesus.

Jesus says, "Listen to me! You can pray for anything, and if you believe, you have it; it's yours! But when you are praying, first forgive anyone you are holding a grudge against, so that your Father in heaven will forgive you your sins too" (Mark 11:24–25, TLB).

When people went to Christ for healing, He taught them to forgive others. Then He would forgive their sins, and they would be made whole. Forgiving those who hurt you is not easy. I have had to do the same thing in my life, and I ran from it for a while. I encourage you to stop running, if you are, and come to Jesus.

Lay your burdened and weary heart at His feet. As you forgive those who abused or hurt you in any way, He will forgive you and give you peace.

> Some people brought to him a paralyzed man on a mat. Seeing their faith, Jesus said to the paralyzed man, "Be encouraged, my child! Your sins are forgiven."... Then Jesus turned to the paralyzed man and said, "Stand up, pick up your mat, and go home!" And the man jumped up and went home!
>
> —MATTHEW 9:2, 6–7

This can be your story too. Can you imagine the joy and peace of living according to God's perfect design for your life?

> Then Jesus said, "Come to me, all of you who are weary and carry heavy burdens, and I will give you rest. Take my yoke upon you. Let me teach you, because I am humble and gentle at heart, and you will find rest for your souls. For my yoke is easy to bear, and the burden I give you is light."
>
> —MATTHEW 11:28–30

2. Abstain from your fleshly desires.

The funny thing is if we don't have sex, we won't die. Many people choose celibacy when they are not married. Think about it. The person addicted to food, resulting in life-threatening illness, also has a problem. She needs to modify her lifestyle. This is often very hard because she can't say, "I'll never eat again." Humans have to eat, or we will die. But oftentimes people jumpstart a new healthy lifestyle with a twenty-one-day sugar detox or a forty-day fast to break their dependency on harmful foods and end unnatural cravings.

Could we not commit ourselves to a season of celibacy, with the season lasting as long as we are not in a God-ordained marriage? This can begin the restoration process of our bodies, minds, and spirits and allow them to come into agreement with God because sex is not only about the body. We must also control our minds, keeping them pure and holy before the Lord. Committing time to pray and fast for freedom from all sorts of sexual sin is a practical way to build up your spirit and reduce the desires of your flesh.

Again, we won't die if we don't have sex. Love and sex are really two different things. Yet we are such a feel-good, gratify-me-now society that we often indulge in things that ultimately cause us to forfeit our health and, in extreme cases, our lives. You can't live in your full potential with spiritual threats looming around you. Abstinence is a good way to give God control.

3. Stay in your own pasture.

My grandfather Daddy King used to preach a sermon called "Nibbling Sweet Grass." It was a parable about a beloved little sheep that ignored his loving master's rule to stay in his own protected pasture. The grass next door in the sheep slaughterer's field appeared to be greener and sweeter. So the little sheep edged closer and closer to the fence, nibbling in ignorant bliss until one day he slipped into the slaughter pen. The rest was history!

This sheep is much like people today. Fornication, adultery, divorce, sexual preference, and so many other lifestyle choices have us out to pasture and in danger. Our sons and daughters value their smartphones, cars, and clothes much more than they value their own bodies, which are the temples of the Holy Ghost. (See 1 Corinthians 6:19.)

Not understanding God's purpose for our lives and bodies breeds the curiosity that led Eve to sin. An example of this is pornography, which entraps so many of our children and adults. Whether it's on the internet, in magazines, or on television, porn is often at the root of perverse sexual exploration. Pornography encourages unholy images and soul ties that are very difficult to break. Porn also leads down the deadly spiraled path to human sex trafficking.

When our minds start to wander into fantasies and to places outside the pasture God has set up for us, it is important that we say no and we reset our minds on things above (Col. 3:2). We need to obey God when He sets boundaries around us and trust that He knows, as Abba, what's best for us.

King Family Truth

Obey God when He sets boundaries around your life, and trust that He knows what's best for you.

4. Apply the blood of Jesus.

The blood of Jesus—that pure DNA of Christ the Lamb—can never lose its power! We need the blood of Jesus to deliver us from temptation. The Bible says that through the blood of Jesus we can be cleansed from all sin:

> But if we are living in the light, as God is in the light, then we have fellowship with each other, and the blood of Jesus, his Son, cleanses us from all sin.
>
> —1 John 1:7

Through the blood of Jesus we have power over the enemy:

> And they have defeated him by the blood of the Lamb and by their testimony.
>
> —Revelation 12:11

I encourage you to pray the previous scriptures over yourself. Jesus came and defeated the works of the devil (1 John 3:8) so you could have access to the throne of God, where you can find supernatural help when you need it (Heb. 4:16).

5. Pull it up from the root.

Without being born again, the human race is subject, or slave, to sin and iniquity. Iniquity breeds sin, and once grown, sin leads to spiritual and physical death. Iniquity is like the soil or fertilizer. Sin is the seed, which once grown brings death. Sin is an evil fruit that must be pulled up from the roots and destroyed by the Word of God, the blood of Jesus, and the power of the Holy Ghost. Too often we attack the symptoms without dealing with the root problems. We mow the grass, as it were, chopping off the tops of the weeds without killing their roots.

Redemption through Christ is needed to free humanity from the curse that results from iniquity and sin. We are not just talking about Christian conversion here. We can be saved and at church every Sunday while still indulging in sin and sickness—yes, *indulging in sickness*. We do this when we participate in sin that will result in sickness and ultimately death. This includes sinning in what we choose to consume, our sexual behavior, and what we do in and away from our homes.

We need to graduate from conversion to deliverance. We need to be free from the generational curses of sin. We need to know the truth, which will set us free! Getting to the root of the issues will bring deliverance and healing, allowing us to be all God designed us to be from the foundation of the world.

SCRIPTURE REFLECTION

Nevertheless, to avoid fornication, let every man have his own wife, and let every woman have her own husband.
—1 CORINTHIANS 7:2, KJV

This explains why a man leaves his father and mother and is joined to his wife...
—GENESIS 2:24 (SEE ALSO EPHESIANS 5:31)

He who finds a wife finds a good thing, and obtains favor from the LORD.

—PROVERBS 18:22, NKJV

PERSONAL REFLECTION

How has the lack of knowledge regarding God's plan for human sexuality affected humanity? How can the "born-again" experience help us in seeking sexual wholeness God's way?

PRAYER

Dear Lord, help me understand Your plan for bringing healing and wholeness to my sexual life. Please give me the love, wisdom, and compassion I need to help others understand Your plan for them as well. May my actions line up with Your Word, that I may be blessed to fulfill Your purpose for my life. In Jesus's name, amen.

Chapter 20

DIVINE
RELATIONSHIPS

There are "friends" who destroy each other, but a
real friend sticks closer than a brother.

—PROVERBS 18:24

M Y SON AND I wrote a song together called "Let Me Explain," for which we recorded a video. During the song a couple experiences a misunderstanding, and the relationship between the young man and young woman is damaged as a result. We chose that theme because miscommunication or a lack of communication are common problems that often lead to breakups. Pastor McNair often taught his congregation that communication and fellowship are critical to making a relationship last, no matter what type of relationship it is, and I couldn't agree more.

I've experienced more broken relationships than lasting ones. My longest and most rewarding relationship has, of course, been with God. He has been with me since before I was born, and as Jesus promises, God will never leave me or forsake me. My next–most rewarding relationship has been with my mother. At the time of this writing we have been sharing some of the most loving and fun moments of our lives together—shopping for hearing aids, visiting the chiropractor, playing with the new babies in our family, enjoying outings for lunch, buying jewelry, and making so many other wonderful memories. Yes, we've had some rocky moments, but all in all we share a wonderful love. Our mutual love for Jesus is our most cherished gift.

The next–most precious relationships I have are with each of my children and grandchildren. Watching my children and grandchildren grow up in Jesus is a pure joy. I only wish all of them had experienced time with my departed relatives: Daddy, Granddaddy, Big Mama, and Uncle ML.

Over the course of my relationships with my family I've had to apply what I've shared about forgiveness to mend fences with relatives while they were still living. The lessons I've learned about forgiveness helped me to understand and appreciate the sacrifices required for living the King family legacy and the value of being grateful for the oasis of joy available to me as I pursued loving relationships with those around me.

We all need relationships. They make our lives richer. Just imagine living in this world without human contact to help you along the journey. It wouldn't be much fun. Understanding the key of divine relationships can open the door to sustainable joy and lasting satisfaction. Such joy can be birthed within our own families if we learn how to love, forgive, and appreciate one another. Such joy can then extend to our relationships with those in our communities, including our churches, social circles, and workplaces.

One thing we do in the King family is spend time together, both in small and larger groups. This is when we can put aside political and social viewpoints and pray, eat, play, and just have fun together.

KING FAMILY TRUTH

"People fail to get along...because they fear each other. They fear each other because they don't know each other. They don't know each other because they have not properly communicated with each other."[1]

—Martin Luther King Jr.

DISCERNING WORTHY RELATIONSHIPS

Mike Murdock is an anointed man of God, respected for his wisdom and insight on various topics related to living the Christian life. Having followed his teachings over the years, I developed a list of characteristics we can use to measure all our relationships to determine whether they are worth investing our time and energy in. Every friendship will have an impact on your life. Each relationship in your life will grow weeds or flowers. This is why every relationship in your life should be clearly defined.

To help you discern whether to invest in a particular relationship, I have compiled a list of twenty-five truths about relationships drawn from Mike Murdock's teaching:

1. Your friends affect your future.

2. Each relationship feeds a weakness or a strength.

3. Each friendship is either comfortable with your present or compatible with your future.

4. Every relationship is a current that sweeps you toward your assignment or moves you away from it.

5. Some relationships can damage you irreparably.

6. Some relationships multiply your wisdom.

7. The purpose of wisdom is to disconnect you from wrong people.

8. Your future is determined by the people you permit near you.

9. When Satan wants to destroy you, he puts a person in your life.

10. When God wants to promote you, He puts a person in your life.

11. Those who are fighting against God will fight against the God in you.

12. Those who despise obedience to God will despise your obedience to God.

13. Those who desire God will recognize the God in you.

14. Those who do not increase you will inevitably decrease you.

15. Those who do not make deposits eventually make withdrawals from you.

16. Each friendship will abort or advance your assignment.

17. The Holy Spirit alone can direct you to the right people, who will assist you in completing your assignment.

18. No relationship is ever insignificant.

19. Intimacy should be earned, not freely given. (Read 1 Thessalonians 5:12–13.)

20. Intimacy should be the reward for proven loyalty. (Read John 15:13–14.)

21. True friendship is a gift, never a demanded requirement. (Read 1 Corinthians 13.)

22. When wrong people leave your life, wrong things stop happening. (Read Jonah 1:15.)

23. When right people enter your life, right things begin to happen. (Read John 4:4–30.)

24. If you fail to guard your own life, you are like a city without walls. (Read Proverbs 25:28.)

25. Failure occurs when the wrong person gets too close. (Read Judges 16:4.)

26. One of the greatest gifts God can give you other than Himself is a friend.

FOUR RELATIONSHIP DEAL BREAKERS

It has often been said that opposites attract. While this is true, certain differences can make it difficult for these opposites to form lasting relational ties where fellowship is a key component. At the center of many disagreements and relationship breakdowns are differing opinions about money, sexuality, politics, and religion.

How often do we hear "my money" or "your money" rather than "our money"? How often do we see relationships break down because of issues surrounding sexuality or the lack thereof? How many households are divided by political or religious differences? While nothing is too hard for God, when there is a lack of unity in these areas, the relationships are likely to be fractured at best and at worst, in need of a miracle to survive. As Amos 3:3 asks, "Can two walk together, except they be agreed?" (KJV).

Healthy communication is a key to keeping all types of relationships healthy. When conflict arises, if the issues can be resolved peacefully and nonviolently, there is hope for unity and reconciliation. In the King family we advocate six steps and six principles that can help people conquer any differences that might otherwise divide them. You can read more about the King Philosophy at the King Center website, http://www.thekingcenter.org/king-philosophy.

Healing broken relationships can lead to healing on many levels. Broken hearts, broken minds, broken bodies, broken spirits, and wounded souls need the master key of divine love applied in order to be restored.

LABELS AND FALSE EXPECTATIONS LEAD TO BROKEN RELATIONSHIPS

Often when we have certain expectations about people we want to relate to and those expectations are not met, we are ready to throw in the towel. Or when people don't conform to the boxes we put them in, we are ready to ditch the relationship. Somehow we expect them to accept our labels to meet our approval.

> Am I therefore become your enemy, because I tell you the truth?
>
> —GALATIANS 4:16, KJV

One area that tends to cause strain in relationships, if not complete disintegration, is politics. In preparing this chapter, I was constantly plagued with the burden that accompanies bearing the conservative label. I tend to resist being confined to a box. The labels of conservative and liberal are just as dangerous and misleading as any other labels. They are ambiguous and subjective, so they don't convey a clear meaning. Then when they are attributed to a person or a group, instant division occurs.

Labels prevent people who often share common beliefs on certain issues from standing with others who may believe some of what the first group believes but not everything. Many times we find that the definitions and values overlap, causing one to wonder if liberal means conservative and vice versa. For instance, there are conservatives and liberals who stand for protecting the lives of our children at all stages of life, beginning at conception and ending at natural death. Pro-life values can be held by both liberals and conservatives.

A friend had an experience that caused her to realize the folly of labeling people.

> We have driven a lot of cars in our day—some new, some used, and some mere relics of what they once were. At one point when our money was low, we purchased a vehicle that came with those wonderful outdated political bumper stickers. There is nothing like running around with a Carter bumper sticker when George Bush Sr. is in office. So,

being naive about the tenacity with which these labels are designed to adhere to the surface on which they are placed, I figured I could apply some elbow grease and chemicals to get the label off.

One morning after breakfast I went forth, armed with my rubber gloves, squeegee, soapy water, and pure ammonia. First I applied the soapy water liberally and then tried to scrub through the label with a sponge. No give. Then I applied pure ammonia, and the only thing that loosed up was the congestion in my head. Next I went into the kitchen for a razor blade, figuring I could gently get the edges to come loose and then ease the rest of the label off. After about twenty minutes of trying this, the only thing that gave were my rubber gloves, which now had so many bits missing that I had to go get another pair.

While I was inside, I grabbed an extension cord and a hair dryer, thinking that if I heated the sticker it might come loose. But it never did budge completely. I was able to get bits and pieces of it off but never the whole thing. It now looked worse than when I started. But since we had only paid $150 for the car and it already had the seats duct-taped, I dried the chrome bumper off and neatly covered the offending bumper sticker with a piece of gray duct tape, calling the morning a wash.

As I sat on the porch sipping my iced tea and rocking back and forth in my chair, a light suddenly came on in my mind. I realized that the morning had not been a futile effort at all. There were scores of lessons to be learned from that old bumper sticker.

First, labels stick. When we as Christians label one another—be it our children, our spouse, or our fellow man—those labels have a tendency to stick. The more we use them, the greater the intensity of the bond between the person and the label becomes. We get tired and frustrated that our toddlers have not yet learned to see what is so obvious to us, and suddenly we call them stupid, dumb, or some other barb that sticks in their minds and begins to grow.

We feel insecure or frightened, so we give groups and organizations brands that portray them as the enemy, and then wonder why we cannot work together or live together in harmony. We view religions, creeds, ethnic groups, and even socioeconomic groups as either acceptable or not by criteria that are often based on fear, insecurity, lies, and sin. Then, after we have wrongfully judged the groups in question, we resort to labeling them with hateful, demeaning, divisive names that stick. Later, when we find a common cause, we struggle to unite yet often fail because of the distrust, deep wounds, and division these labels have bred within us. Labels stick.

Secondly, labels are hard to remove. Sadly we often realize our mistake after the toddler has become a young adult. He has grown up hearing us berate him in anger, with labels that each year ingrained a false understanding of himself into the fiber of his heart and character until finally, when we wake up and see what we have done, the damage is so deeply rooted it will not easily be removed. The economy is a problem, there are rumors of war, and poverty is rampant and spreading. As a society we need to come together to solve these problems, but the labels are stuck. We don't trust each other. We don't see each other in the light of what we can become but rather in the archaic and hateful labels we have grown up to embrace.

So then our collaborations are weak when we need them to be strong, and we find standing together for a good cause difficult to nearly impossible when it should be so easy. We want to trust one another, but the labels are sticking. We want to be fearless, but the labels are sticking. We want to forgive one another, but the labels have bonded deep into our hearts. We want to unite, but there are so many divisions, and the labels just will not give. Labels are hard to remove.

Thirdly, sometimes we just have to put a patch on it and try to move forward in hopes that time will heal. The patch is not pretty. The beauty of the sparkling, polished chrome bumper on our car will be forever marred by the patch, but gradually, over time, things change. The bumper gets old and starts peeling and rusting, and suddenly a duct tape patch doesn't stand out so much. But it takes a lot of time, and, sadly, while we can move forward, there will always be some damage left behind.

Labels prevent us from loving one another as God has commanded us to. Labels inhibit us from doing unto others as we would have them do unto us. Labels hinder us from allowing the fruit of the Spirit to flow from our hearts to those around us. Labels ostracize people who are created in God's image and cause us to do what God says is foolish— judging ourselves by others rather than by the law of God. Labels impede the movements of unity, peace, and harmony, for which our families, our communities, our nation, and our world are pleading.

Labels are something Christians must avoid at all costs. After all, the bumper stickers we are applying in our daily lives are adhered to human hearts, not mere cars or buildings. The bond and the subsequent damage run deep and affect not only individuals but families, communities, and nations for generation after generation. The use of labels *must* stop immediately. This is something I think of every time I see a bumper sticker.[2]

Labels are divisive, boxes are restrictive, and they hurt our connection to one another. This is why I resist the label of conservative.

The practice of accepting and assigning labels and boxes is just as bad as separating people based on race. This practice is deceptive and dangerous. We are one human race, not separate races and classes divided by skin color. There is no red, black, white, brown, or yellow race. There is one human race with ethnic distinctions, so when we put people in a color box, we begin to discriminate, which is sin.

Another practice of labeling and boxing is restricting God-given gifts that emerge in people we have stereotyped. For example, can an accountant not also be a poet? Can a scientist not also be a great cook? When we label people according to our understanding of their gifts and talents, we leave no room for God's creativity to burst forth in multiple streams. I have a friend who is a real estate and investment genius. Yet he also is a wonderful composer and producer of music. People often tell him that his music is a nice hobby but he should stick to one thing. How sad!

KING FAMILY TRUTH

"Peace is not merely a distant goal that we seek, but a means by which we arrive at that goal."[3]

—Martin Luther King Jr

In the Beloved Community, embraced by our family and broadly proclaimed by my uncle ML, labels, boxes, and separate races don't exist. Instead, relationships are formed and nurtured with the agape love of God. Ours is a community that seeks harmony and liberty tempered with righteous living, where everyone agrees to seek and believe God for a world where agape love is supreme and healthy relationships abound.

SCRIPTURE REFLECTION

How good and pleasant it is when God's people live together in unity!

—PSALM 133:1, NIV

PERSONAL REFLECTION

Are there three relationships you would like to work on right now? Write them down, and reflect on ways to improve them.

PRAYER

Lord, help me understand and desire healthy relationships in my life and do my part in developing them. This I pray in Jesus's name. Amen.

Chapter 21

DIVINE CONNECTIONS

I have observed something else under the sun. The fastest
runner doesn't always win the race, and the strongest warrior
doesn't always win the battle. The wise sometimes go hungry,
and the skillful are not necessarily wealthy. And those who
are educated don't always lead successful lives. It is all decided
by chance, by being in the right place at the right time.

—ECCLESIASTES 9:11

THE BIBLE IS full of unexpected moments. Some events seem almost coincidental, where people are in the right place at the right time. Did Jesus just happen by the well when the Samaritan woman was there? No. That was a divine connection. Did Esther just happen to be noticed by the king's search party? No, hers was a divine appointment. Did Joseph just happen to be tossed into a pit by his brothers? No. He was being groomed to become their deliverer.

We meet people in unlikely and ordinary places, under both normal and unusual circumstances. We use terms such as *déjà vu, serendipity,* and *happenstance* to try to account for connections with people that somehow change our lives. But it is hard to articulate with our limited vocabulary the very special ways God uses divine connections to launch us into our destiny.

I used to categorize unexpected encounters in such limited terms, but the time came when I began to open my life to the infinite ways of God and to live in a constant state of believing for and expecting the unexpected to happen in almost any place at any time. Nothing happens by accident, not even the graceful float of a butterfly on a lovely summer day, bringing to our awareness a poetic phrase that then becomes a song.

In the introduction to this book I alluded to the fact that completing this book has been perhaps one of the hardest adventures in my life. I keep moving back and forth across the manuscript, through the divine keys, realizing that it is taking so long because God is constantly downloading more content to me through the experience of everyday living.

Of course my every day is not your every day, and vice versa. We are uniquely and wonderfully made. So we are different. And yet there are similarities and common "spaces" where we intersect. This takes us back to divine connections and being in the right place at the right time.

How to Know Where to Be Blessed

A key point in developing the knack of being in the perfect space and atmosphere for divine connections and blessings is the cultivation of the habit of "inquiring of the Lord." The psalmist says, "One thing I have asked from the LORD, that will I seek after—for me to dwell in the house of the LORD all the days of my life, to see the beauty of the LORD, and to inquire in His temple" (Ps. 27:4, MEV). Discovering where you need to be to connect with the unexpected things of God has to do with asking God for directions. Psalm 119:133 says, "Guide my steps by your word, so I will not be overcome by evil."

Faith is also a primary factor in being just where God wants us at the right time. Throughout this book we have been discovering that our spiritual keys can bring us closer to God. As we draw near to God, the divine moments in our lives increase, and we begin living in His presence, the atmosphere where miracles become our reality.

In Hebrews 11 we see that faith caused people to move into God's plan for their lives. While seeking and obeying God's will, they experienced miracles that many can only long for. They were in the right place at the right time.

An impression, thought, or nudge to stop by a certain place not on your usual schedule—such as a store, community meeting, or church service—can be the Holy Spirit leading you to a divine connection. Yes, these off-the-beaten-path experiences are often divine connections. As Oswald Chambers wrote, "Wherever God puts you in circumstances, pray immediately, pray that His Atonement may be realized in other lives as it has been in yours.

Pray for your friends now; pray for those with whom you come in contact now."[1]

PUT YOUR AGENDA ON THE BACK BURNER

Divine connections come when we allow room for them in our lives. Sometimes when I'm busy doing my thing, someone will call with an idea or something they want to promote. People call me with suggestions to meet someone new, contact someone from my past, consider a new project, and countless other things. I used to put such outreaches off, thinking I was too busy to be bothered. However, over time I began to put my natural schedule and agenda on the back burner as I began to pray over every contact I made.

Doors began to open up. What seemed like coincidences proved to be road maps. The cliché "It's a small world" became a reality. I was meeting people connected to other people I already knew, had contact with, or had met before. In prayer I began to realize that these were divine connections. I began to see every contact, every stop I didn't predetermine as an encounter God could use in my life. These God encounters are not serendipity, happenstance, or coincidence. They are divine connections.

Having met so many people in so many places—people considered very influential and those who are virtually unknown—I have come to learn that God's ways are not our ways; His thoughts are not our thoughts (Isa. 55:8). That "annoying" person in your life who always calls at the "wrong" time, who wants you to stop doing something important to you so you can do something that is seemingly useless—that could be someone God is using to open doors for you. Of course discernment is key in such instances. People and things can also be serious distractions that take us off the divine path.

King Family Truth

There's a right time and place for everything.

The Right Place at the Right Time

As I mentioned previously, I've been honored to serve God with different gifts and in different roles. I was so inspired by the fact that God aligns our lives with His perfect timing to bless us and move us into our calling that I wrote a poem about this titled "The Right Place, the Right Time." I pray it inspires you to believe for and welcome the unexpected divine connections God brings into your life.

> It's the right time; it's the right place
>   as we run this human race.
> There's a reason
>   this is my season.
> It's not serendipity,
>   God's plan for me.
> It's not happenstance.
>   No circumstance
>   can hold me down,
>   for God's grace abounds
>   toward me.
>
> Divine appointments happen every day.
> Divine connections connect us to eternity.
> There's a right time and place, for everything.
> Sage wisdom.
>
> This is my season
>   and there's a reason
>   for what keeps happening
>   in my life.

It's about my purpose,
    and all connecting,
        being in the right place at the right time.

We meet people all the time,
    in familiar and unchartered places.
    Going through these spaces
    we don't quite connect the dots
    to see what hides
    beneath the faces
    in the spaces
    where we meet.

Peripherals collide and convergence is imminent;
    still we cry coincidence and déjà vu.
    If we pause for our reflections and seek the reasons why
      our paths take new directions,
    we still have intersections
    that reach past our human minds.

These far and close encounters are not by accident;
    there is purpose and there is destiny ahead.
Logic says coincidence breeds near and far encounters;
    déjà vu too.
Yet logic is not the final authority.
    Again, it's not serendipity;
    it's divine.
    It's being in the right place at the right time.

I love the way Matthew 2:9–10, as translated in *The Message* Bible, confirms the words of this poem:

> Instructed by the king, they set off. Then the star appeared again, the same star they had seen in the eastern skies. It led them on until it hovered over the place of the child. They

could hardly contain themselves: They were in the right place! They had arrived at the right time!

God Determines Our Destinies

As we close these chapters on the keys to unlocking our spiritual potential, we must be ever grateful for the incredible sacrifice God made for us to become not only His creations but also His children. We are children of God and heirs to His kingdom, and He determines our destinies. He has given us keys to His kingdom, and we have the power and authority to triumph over all the works of the enemy so our paths to living in our full potential are clear.

Scripture Reflection

We can make our plans, but the Lord determines our steps.
—Proverbs 16:9

Personal Reflection

How often do you go about your day in a hurry, without recognizing or acknowledging God's presence operating in your life to complete a good work in you? Make a journal, and record recognizable "acts of God" in your ordinary goings-on.

Prayer

Heavenly Father, thank You for guiding my actions in life, always directing me to the right place at the right time. Help me hear and obey and receive Your blessings more and more. This I pray in Jesus's name. Amen.

NOTES

FOREWORD

1.   I believe that there are many good police officers, and I am deeply grateful for their service. My intention is not to cast blame on the police forces in general but to tell real stories from my friend's past.

2.   Charlayne Hunter-Gault, "Fifty Years After the Birmingham Children's Crusade," *New Yorker*, May 2, 2013, accessed October 24, 2017, https://www.newyorker.com/news/news-desk/fifty-years-after-the -birmingham-childrens-crusade.

3.   Eric Metaxas, *Martin Luther* (New York: Viking Press, 2017), 1.

INTRODUCTION

1.   *English Oxford Living Dictionaries*, s.v. "authority," accessed September 26, 2017, https://en.oxforddictionaries.com/definition /authority.

2.   *English Oxford Living Dictionaries*, s.v. "power," accessed September 26, 2017, https://en.oxforddictionaries.com/definition/power.

CHAPTER 1: DIVINE LOVE—THE MASTER KEY

1.   Strong's Concordance, s.v. *"agapē,"* accessed September 27, 2017, https://www.blueletterbible.org/lang/lexicon/lexicon.cfm?Strongs =G26&t=KJV.

2.   "Types of Love," The Bible Study Site, accessed September 27, 2017, http://www.biblestudy.org/question/what-are-three-types-of-love-in -new-testament.html.

3.   "MLK Quote of the Week: Sticking to Love," The King Center, November 16, 2012, http://www.thekingcenter.org/blog/mlk-quote-week -sticking-love.

4.   Jennie B. Wilson, "Hold to God's Unchanging Hand," 1906, http://library.timelesstruths.org/music/Hold_to_Gods_Unchanging _Hand/. Public domain.

CHAPTER 2: DIVINE SALVATION

1. Lindsay Terry, *I Could Sing of Your Love Forever* (Nashville, TN: Thomas Nelson, 2008), 207–208.

2. Martin Luther King Jr., *A Gift of Love: Sermons From Strength to Love and Other Preachings* (Boston, MA: Beacon Press, 2012), 18.

3. From "How Should a Christian View Communism," quoted in James P. Stobaugh, *Studies in World History Volume 3 (Student): The Modern Age to Present* (Green Forest, AR: Master Books, 2014), 76.

CHAPTER 3: DIVINE FORGIVENESS

1. Martin Luther King Jr., "Loving Your Enemies," August 31, 1952 (estimated), https://kinginstitute.stanford.edu/king-papers/documents /loving-your-enemies.

2. "The King Philosophy," The King Center, accessed October 8, 2017, http://www.thekingcenter.org/king-philosophy.

3. "Open Letter: The Beloved Community and the Unborn," Priests for Life, accessed October 11, 2017, http://www.priestsforlife.org /africanamerican/sign-aao-letter.aspx?id=53.

4. Martin Luther King Jr., "Remaining Awake Through a Great Revolution," Electronic Oberlin Group, June 1965, http://www2.oberlin .edu/external/EOG/BlackHistoryMonth/MLK/CommAddress.html.

CHAPTER 4: DIVINE AUTHORITY

1. Mary Kassian, "7 Misconceptions About Submission," Girls Gone Wise, accessed October 11, 2017, https://girlsgonewise.com/7 -misconceptions-about-submission/.

2. Kassian, "7 Misconceptions About Submission."

3. Martin Luther King Jr., "Paul's Letter to American Christians," The Martin Luther King Jr. Research and Education Institute, November 4, 1956, http://kingencyclopedia.stanford.edu/encyclopedia/document sentry/doc_pauls_letter_to_american_christians.1.html.

CHAPTER 5: DIVINE GRACE AND MERCY

1. "Grace," Bible Gateway, accessed October 8, 2017, https://www .biblegateway.com/quicksearch/?quicksearch=grace&qs_version=KJV.

2. *English Oxford Living Dictionaries*, s.v. "grace," accessed October 8, 2017, https://en.oxforddictionaries.com/definition/grace.

3. *English Oxford Living Dictionaries*, s.v. "grace."

4. English Oxford *Living Dictionaries*, s.v. "mercy," accessed October 8, 2017, https://en.oxforddictionaries.com/definition/us/mercy.

5.   Oswald Chambers, "Drawing on the Grace of God—Now," My Utmost for His Highest, accessed October 8, 2017, https://utmost.org/drawing-on-the-grace-of-god%E2%80%94-now/.

6.   Kim Lawton, "Wintley Phipps," PBS.org, November 24, 2009, http://www.pbs.org/wnet/religionandethics/2009/11/24/november-27-2009-wintley-phipps/5110/.

7.   Lawton, "Wintley Phipps."

8.   Lawton, "Wintley Phipps."

9.   "Amazing Grace," Hymnal.net, accessed October 8, 2017, https://www.hymnal.net/en/hymn/h/313.

Chapter 6: Divine Faith

1.   In communication with the author.

Chapter 7: Divine Obedience

1.   Oswald Chambers, "How Will I Know?," My Utmost for His Highest, accessed October 8, 2017, https://utmost.org/how-will-i-know/.

2.   In communication with the author.

3.   Dictionary.com, s.v. "submit," accessed October 8, 2017, http://www.dictionary.com/browse/submit?s=t.

4.   Dictionary.com, s.v. "obey," accessed October 8, 2017, http://www.dictionary.com/browse/obey?s=t.

5.   Sunny Shell, "Difference Between Submission and Obedience," My Second Love, accessed October 8, 2017, http://www.mysecondlove.net/2008/08/difference-between-submission-and.html#WX_jDtPythE.

Chapter 8: Divine Submission

1.   Kassian, "7 Misconceptions About Submission."

2.   Kassian, "7 Misconceptions About Submission."

3.   Kassian, "7 Misconceptions About Submission."

4.   Alveda C. King, *I Don't Want Your Man, I Want My Own* (n.p.: Lushena Books, 2001).

Chapter 9: Divine Surrender

1.   Dictionary.com, s.v. "surrender," accessed October 8, 2017, http://www.dictionary.com/browse/surrender.

2.   Dictionary.com, s.v. "surrender."

3.   Dictionary.com, s.v. "surrender."

4.   Will L. Thompson, "Softly and Tenderly Jesus Is Calling," 1880, https://hymnary.org/text/softly_and_tenderly_jesus_is_calling. Public domain.

5. Oswald Chambers, "After Surrender—What?," My Utmost for His Highest, accessed October 8, 2017, https://utmost.org/classic/after-surrender-what-classic/.

6. Chambers, "After Surrender—What?"

7. Chambers, "After Surrender—What?"

CHAPTER 10: DIVINE HUMILITY

1. *Merriam-Webster*, s.v. "humility," accessed October 8, 2017, https://www.merriam-webster.com/dictionary/humility; *English Oxford Living Dictionaries*, s.v. "humility," accessed October 8, 2017, https://en.oxforddictionaries.com/definition/humility.

2. In communication with the author.

3. Martin Luther King Jr., "The Drum Major Instinct," The King Center, 1968, http://www.thekingcenter.org/get-involved.

4. In communication with the author.

CHAPTER 11: DIVINE PRAYER

1. William W. Walford, "Sweet Hour of Prayer," 1845, http://library.timelesstruths.org/music/Sweet_Hour_of_Prayer/. Public domain.

2. In communication with the author, September 2017.

3. For more on how God works through prayer, see John D. Barry and Rebecca Van Noord, "July 17: Emotion Versus Logic," *Connect the Testaments* (Bellingham, WA: Lexham Press, 2014).

CHAPTER 12: DIVINE PRAISE AND WORSHIP

1. S. Elaine Clay, *Born to Sing Songs of Deliverance* (Maitland, FL: Xulon Press, 2016), 37–38.

2. Dean Mitchum, "Finding the Right Mix for Your Prophetic Psalmist Reputation," The Elijah List, April 23, 2016, http://www.elijahlist.com/words/display_word.html?ID=15984. Used by permission.

CHAPTER 13: DIVINE PROPHECY

1. Dictionary.com, s.v. "prophecy," accessed October 8, 2017, http://www.dictionary.com/browse/prophecy.

2. Martin Luther King Jr., "I've Been to the Mountaintop," The Martin Luther King Jr. Research and Education Institute, April 3, 1968, http://kingencyclopedia.stanford.edu/encyclopedia/documentsentry/ive_been_to_the_mountaintop/.

3. Charlotte Baker, *The Eye of the Needle and Other Prophetic Parables* (n.p.: McDougal Publishing Company, 1997). Used by permission.

CHAPTER 14: DIVINE UNDERSTANDING

1. The following revelation of the origins of race and ethnicity follows the research presented in John L. Johnson, *The Black Biblical Heritage* (Nashville, TN: Winston-Derek Publishers Inc., 1994). Updated and edited for this publication, it was originally published in Alveda King, *Who We Are in Christ Jesus* (Bloomington, IN: Xlibris, 2008).

2. Jane Gitschier, "All About Mitochondrial Eve: An Interview With Rebecca Cann," PLOS Genetics, May 27, 2010, http://journals.plos .org/plosgenetics/article?id=10.1371%2Fjournal.pgen.1000959.

3. Tia Ghose, "'Out of Africa' Story Being Rewritten Again," LiveScience, March 21, 2013, https://www.livescience.com/28086-when -humans-left-africa.html.

4. William Dwight McKissic Sr., *Beyond Roots: In Search of Blacks in the Bible* (Wenonah, NY: Renaissance Productions, 1990), 17–18.

5. "The Jew and the Gentile: Background of the Jew in the Old Testament," Bible.org, accessed October 9, 2017, https://bible.org/series page/6-jew-and-gentile-background-jew-old-testament.

6. "The Jew and the Gentile," Bible.org.

7. Bodie Hodge and Tommy Mitchell, "Noah, a Global Flood, and the Case Against Racism," Answers in Genesis, June 22, 2007, https:// answersingenesis.org/racism/noah-a-global-flood-and-the-case-against -racism/.

8. "What Does It Mean to Be Human," Smithsonian National Museum of Natural History, accessed October 9, 2017, http://human origins.si.edu/evidence/genetics/human-skin-color-variation/modern -human-diversity-skin-color.

9. Johnson, *The Black Biblical Heritage*, 51.

10. Johnson, *The Black Biblical Heritage*, 81.

11. "King Solomon and the Queen of Sheba," Grace Thru Faith, December 1, 2012, https://gracethrufaith.com/ask-a-bible-teacher/king -solomon-and-the-queen-of-sheba/.

12. Amos 9:7; Zephaniah 3:10; E. A. Wallis Budge, *Kebra Nagast: The Queen of Sheba and Her Only Son Menyelek* (Boston, MA: British Museum, 1922).

13. "Falasha," Encyclopaedia Britannica, accessed October 9, 2017, https://www.britannica.com/topic/Falasha.

14. "Africa Virtual Jewish History Tour," Jewish Virtual Library, October 9, 2017, https://www.jewishvirtuallibrary.org/africa-virtual -jewish-history-tour.

15. Gloria Levitas, "How to Be Black and Jewish," *Moment* magazine, December 28, 2012, http://www.momentmag.com/book-review -black-jews-in-africa-and-the-americas/; see also Tudor Parfitt, *Black Jews*

in Africa and the Americas (Boston, MA: Harvard University Press, 2013).

CHAPTER 15: DIVINE LIFE

1.   "Abortion Statistics," National Right to Life, accessed October 9, 2017, http://www.nrlc.org/uploads/factsheets/FS01AbortionintheUS.pdf.

2.   "Abortion Surveillance—United States, 1995," CDC, accessed October 9, 2017, https://www.cdc.gov/mmwr/preview/mmwrhtml /00053774.htm; see also "CDC: 35% of Aborted Babies Are Black," LifeSite, December 5, 2016, https://www.lifesitenews.com/news/cdc -statistics-indicate-abortion-rate-continues-to-be-higher-among-minoriti.

3.   Martin Luther King Jr., *The Trumpet of Conscience* (San Francisco: Harper and Row, 1967), 72.

4.   Glenn Kessler, "Margaret Sanger, Planned Parenthood and Black Abortions: Ben Carson's False Claim," *Washington Post*, August 18, 2015, https://www.washingtonpost.com/news/fact-checker/wp/2015/08/18 /carsons-claim-that-planned-parenthood-targets-blacks-to-control-that -population/?utm_term=.d840d0111a20.

5.   "The Abortion-Breast Cancer Link," LifeSite, accessed October 9, 2017, https://www.lifesitenews.com/resources/abortion/the-abortion -breast-cancer-link; see also "Abortion Risks," Foothills Pregnancy Resource Center, accessed October 9, 2017, http://www.foothillsprc.org /risks.php.

6.   Vijaya Kumar, *The World's Greatest Speeches* (New York: Sterling Publishers, 2013), 173.

7.   Martin Luther King III, *The Words of Martin Luther King Jr.* (New York: William Morrow Paperbacks, 2001).

CHAPTER 16: DIVINE JUSTICE

1.   Millard J. Erickson, *Christian Theology* (Grand Rapids, MI: Baker Academic, 2013).

2.   Paul P. Enns, *The Moody Handbook of Theology* (Chicago, IL: Moody Publishers, 2008).

3.   "The King Philosophy," The King Center, accessed October 9, 2017, http://www.thekingcenter.org/king-philosophy.

4.   Merriam-Webster.com, s.v. "dichotomous key," accessed October 9, 2017, https://www.merriam-webster.com/dictionary/dichotomous%20 key.

5.   Merriam-Webster.com, s.v. "dichotomous," accessed October 9, 2017, https://www.merriam-webster.com/dictionary/dichotomous.

6.   Monnica T. Williams, PhD, "Colorblind Ideology Is a Form of Racism," PsychologyToday.com, December 27, 2011, accessed October 9, 2017, https://www.psychologytoday.com/blog/culturally-speaking/201112 /colorblind-ideology-is-form-racism.

7.   Tim Wise, "F.A.Q.s: What Do You Mean by White Privilege?," TimWise.org, accessed October 9, 2017, http://www.timwise.org/f-a-q-s/. Used by permission.

8.   Wise, "F.A.Q.s: What Do You Mean by White Privilege?"

9.   Wise, "F.A.Q.s: What Do You Mean by White Privilege?"

10.   0. Jordan Ballor, "The Hearts and Habits of Men: MLK on Law and Morality," For the Life of the World, January 19, 2016, accessed October 9, 2017, http://www.letterstotheexiles.com/hearts-habits-men -mlk-law-morality/.

CHAPTER 17: DIVINE FAMILY

1.   Denny Cline, "A Key to Revival: Restore the Family," The Elijah List, April 16, 2016, accessed October 9, 2017, http://www.elijahlist.com /words/display_word.html?ID=15958.

CHAPTER 18: DIVINE INTIMACY

1.   Oswald Chambers, "The Nature of Regeneration," My Utmost for His Highest, accessed October 9, 2017, https://utmost.org/the-nature-of -regeneration/.

2.   King, A Gift of Love, 148.

3.   Oswald Chambers, "What Are You Haunted By?," My Utmost for His Highest, accessed October 9, 2017, https://utmost.org/classic/ what-are-you-haunted-by-classic/.

4.   John D. Barry, "June 1: What Wealth Reveals," Ezekiel Count-down, June 1, 2017, https://ezekielcountdown.wordpress.com/2017/06/01 /connect-the-testaments-232/.

CHAPTER 19: DIVINE SEXUALITY

1.   For advice on how to talk with a child who says he's gay, visit Focus on the Family, "Responding to Teen Child Who Says He's Gay," accessed November 10, 2017, http://www.focusonthefamily.com/family -q-and-a/sexuality/responding-to-teen-child-who-says-hes-gay. See also David Murray, "'Mom, Dad…I'm Gay.' A Christian Parent's Response," Christianity.com, accessed November 10, 2017, http://www.christianity .com/christian-life/marriage-and-family/mom-dad-i-m-gay-a-christian -parent-s-response.html.

2. Martin Luther King Jr., "Advice for Living," The Martin Luther King Jr. Research and Education Institute, January 1958, http://king encyclopedia.stanford.edu/encyclopedia/documentsentry/advice_for _living4.1.html.

3. Martin Luther King Jr., "Advice for Living," The Martin Luther King Jr. Research and Education Institute, June 1958, http://king encyclopedia.stanford.edu/encyclopedia/documentsentry/advice_for _living9.1.html.

4. Alveda C. King, "Human Sexuality: It All Started With an Apple," Priests for Life, January 13, 2015, http://www.priestsforlife.org /africanamerican/5154-and-it-all-started-with-an-apple.

Chapter 20: Divine Relationships

1. Martin Luther King Jr., "Advice for Living," The Martin Luther King Jr. Research and Education Institute, May 1958, http://king encyclopedia.stanford.edu/encyclopedia/documentsentry/advice_for _living8.1.html.

2. Adapted from Dr. Alveda C. King with Elizabeth Stoner, "Shedding the Labels and Boxes, Embracing the Truth," Priests for Life, April 1, 2009, http://www.priestsforlife.org/library/document-print.aspx?ID=5807.

3. Martin Luther King Jr., "The Casualties of the War in Vietnam," Speeches and Sounds, February 25, 1967, http://www.aavw.org/special _features/speeches_speech_king02.html.

Chapter 21: Divine Connections

1. Oswald Chambers, "Have You Come to 'When' Yet?," My Utmost for His Highest, accessed October 10, 2017, https://utmost.org /classic/2854-classic/.

CONNECT WITH US!

CHARISMA HOUSE

(Spiritual Growth)

Facebook.com/CharismaHouse

@CharismaHouse

Instagram.com/CharismaHouse

(Health)

Pinterest.com/CharismaHouse

MODERN ENGLISH VERSION

(Bible)

www.mevbible.com

Within each generation emerge select men and women of faith who define their times. They are unique specimen images of the Creator who are divinely designed to steer the historical rudders of change. These kingdom pioneers soar high above and beyond the familiar platitudes of conformity to bring heaven to earth. Even so, my beloved sister Alveda King is one such remarkable agent of social and kingdom transformation who is leading in the front lines as we prepare the way of the Lord. She is supernaturally empowered with love, courage, and wisdom. She is the living fulfillment of a saint overflowing with the abundance of grace and truth. In this book Alveda reduces the mystery of powerful, life-changing spiritual keys to simple precepts of faith in action that can be apprehended by anyone who dares to believe and activate them in their daily walk. This book is a must-read, a treasured gift to the body of Christ, as one considers the ultimate price that she and her family have paid to uncover the keys that unlock the mysteries of divine truths.

—FRANK AMEDIA
COFOUNDER, TOUCH HEAVEN MINISTRIES

King Truths is a must-read for all people who want to understand the deeper meanings of grace and life in Christ. Taking an inside peek at the King family legacy with the eyes of faith will allow any individual, group, or church to come to a realistic conclusion: that God loves family!

—LEON BENJAMIN
NEW LIFE HARVEST CHURCH, RICHMOND, VIRGINIA

Dr. Alveda C. King has been speaking truth in love for decades now—a legacy she now carries from her famous uncle and civil rights icon Dr. Martin Luther King Jr. In her latest great read, *King Truths: 21 Keys to Unlocking Your Spiritual Potential*, Alveda shares the legacy with relevancy and challenges us all to go deeper. What will your legacy be? How will you achieve it? What gifts and talents will you unearth for the benefit of others, and how will your children, your community, and your nation be impacted by the truths you have chosen for your own life? For believers and nonbelievers alike, evangelist Alveda King has proved the relevancy of King truths in her own life and beckons you to know, as she does, the greatest truth teller of them all—Jesus Christ, the King of kings!

—Jensine Bard
Founder and CEO, Jensine Bard Ministries Inc.

It is with great honor that I endorse the timely and needed words of Alveda King written in this book. Alveda has been given the gift of articulation to communicate the truths of the Word of God as they apply to the events of the day—simply said, words written and spoken to give understanding of "on earth as it is in heaven." In *King Truths* are timeless words and wisdom that give hope, healing, life, and needed clarity to the times we live in.

—Cindy Collins
SpeakHope.net

In her new book, *King Truths*, Dr. Alveda King has an amazing way of making her readers want what she has, which is not only true knowledge and love of our Father God but also the love and peace of salvation in our Savior Jesus Christ. *King Truths* will unlock an amazing journey to spiritual fulfillment. I want that.

—Day Gardner
The National Black Pro-Life Union

Dr. Alveda King not only carries the activist, civil rights mantle of her uncle Dr. Martin Luther King Jr., but she also has discovered her own unique anointing and gifting. From the bowels of the Scriptures and her own journey of self-discovery, she offers all of us much-needed guidance in finding our own paths, our own voices, and our own unique destinies. This is a must-read for believers of all ages.

—Harry Jackson
Senior Pastor, Hope Christian Church